LEVERHULME PRIMARY PROJECT

The Leverhulme Primary Project is a major research programme into primary teacher education, based at Exeter University. It is directed by Professor Neville Bennett and Professor Ted Wragg and coordinated by Clive Carré.

Ted Wragg is Professor of Education and Director of the School of Education at Exeter University. He has broadcast frequently on educational matters on both radio and television, and is a frequent contributor to magazines and newspapers, including a regular column in the Times Educational Supplement. His many publications include *Teacher Appraisal: A Practical Guide* (1987); *Education in the Market Place* (1988); and *Schools and Parents* (1989).

Neville Bennett is Professor of Primary Education at Exeter University. He has directed a large number of important research projects and has published widely in the field of teaching and learning in primary education. His recent publications include *Recent Advances in Classroom Research* (1985); *A Good Start? Four Year Olds in School* (1989); and *From Special to Ordinary* (1989).

Elisabeth Dunne is a research fellow within the Leverhulme Primary Project. She has taught in middle schools and has extensive research experience on language in the primary classroom. She has contributed to both in-service and initial teacher education and has published reading materials for slow learners.

Clive Carré is coordinator of the Leverhulme Primary Project and series editor for both the *Classroom Skills* and *Curriculum Series*. He has taught science at primary and secondary levels and has worked with teachers in language and learning programmes and on science courses in many parts of the world. He has written and acted as a consultant on science materials in the UK, Australia and Canada.

LPP is part of the Centre for Research on Teaching and Learning

Classroom Skills Series [Series editor: Clive Carré]

Talking and Learning in Groups	Elizabeth Dunne & Neville Bennett
Assessment for Learning	Richard Dunne
Effective Teaching	Ted Wragg & Richard Dunne
Class Management	Ted Wragg
Explaining	George Brown & Ted Wragg
Questioning	Ted Wragg & George Brown

Curriculum Series [Series editor: Clive Carré]

Science	Clive Carré
Mathematics	Richard Dunne
English	David Wray
History and Humanities	Angela Horton & Jon Nichol
Physical Education	Martin Underwood
Cross-curricular Themes	Ted Wragg & Clive Carré
Information Technology	Niki Davis

Leverhulme Primary Project ■ Classroom Skills Series

Series editor
Clive Carré

TALKING AND LEARNING IN GROUPS

Elisabeth Dunne and Neville Bennett

Macmillan Education

First edition 1990

Published by
MACMILLAN EDUCATION LTD
Houndmills, Basingstoke, Hampshire RG21 2XS
and London
Companies and representatives
throughout the world

Printed in Great Britain by
Cathedral Press Ltd, Salisbury, Wilts

British Library Cataloguing in Publication Data
Dunne, Elisabeth
Talking and learning in groups. – (Talking and learning series).
1. England. Primary schools. Teachers. Professional education.
I. Title II. Bennett, Neville *1937-* III. Series 370.71220942

ISBN 0-333-55180-X

Photocopiable material
The following pages contain photocopiable material:
pp 5-6; 25; 30; 44-45; 47.

CONTENTS

*appropriate sheets may be photocopied

PREFACE

The contents of this series of books are based on the research of the Leverhulme Primary Project. This three-year research programme into various aspects of primary teacher education was funded by the Leverhulme Trust and carried out at the University of Exeter.

The books appear in two series. The first can be regarded as a 'skills' series and communicates directly the results of our research programme. The second complements the first series and examines how teachers teach particular subjects, within the context of the National Curriculum. They are designed to help experienced teachers and student-teachers develop professionally; each book focuses upon a specific aspect of teaching skills. They will be useful for:

practising teachers
student teachers
college and university tutors
school-based in-service coordinators
advisory teachers

You may use this book in a number of ways.

You can use it as part of a course on professional studies, or as part of an in-service programme in school. Students and experienced teachers can share ideas about their classroom practice by responding to suggestions made in the books; examples of children's work and recordings of classroom talk can be discussed. The real value of this way of working is that theoretical ideas are discussed within specific contexts which you have helped to create.

Alternatively you can read the text on your own, and reflect on the various skills and teaching strategies suggested, in terms of your own classroom practice. Having read parts of the book, you may wish to try out some of the ideas with a class of children. The experience of trying to put into practice some of these ideas and then being self-critical about your efforts will develop your teaching skills.

These books will assist in bringing about change at a classroom level and at managerial levels will help decision-making towards whole school policies.

All books have suggested activities which have been tried out by teachers and those in pre-service training; their comments have been acknowledged and acted upon.

We hope both series will provoke discussion, help you to reflect on your current practice and encourage you to ask questions about everyday classroom events.

Clive Carré

ACKNOWLEDGEMENTS

The writing of this book would not have been possible without the many teachers that we have worked with over the last few years. Their suggestions, reflections and ideas have further stimulated our own thinking on improving groupwork and have refined and improved the activities within this book.

Introduction
AIMS AND CONTENT

This book is about changing your classroom practice. We are not pushing a teaching approach that is impossible to manage, or 'another terrific idea' devoid of theoretical support or classroom evaluation. Instead our aim is to allow you to set up effective cooperative groupwork by giving you the necessary rationale, knowledge and skills to do so. These are linked to a series of classroom activities presented in a sequence designed to take you, step by step, towards implementing it yourself.

Several of the ideas in this book may be new to you, but the idea of children working in groups will certainly not be. Unfortunately, as we shall see, most classroom groups are not cooperative, and fall short of the aspirations that the Plowden Report, for example, envisaged nearly a quarter of a century ago. This report was very enthusiastic about the benefits to children, both socially and intellectually, of working collaboratively. We present evidence in the book in support of these views. Furthermore our work over several years with teachers, over the full primary age range, has provided additional evidence that children's learning and social relationships can substantially be enhanced by this approach. However, we do not claim that cooperative grouping is a panacea, or that it should be used all the time, but we do believe that classrooms can be more lively, exciting and effective places for learning through such means.

We have tried, wherever possible, to avoid jargon. However, this has not always proved possible because some technical language is a useful, and understandable, shorthand; for example, we use the term 'post-task interview' to save writing, each time, – 'after the children had finished their work we talked to them in order to ascertain the extent to which they had understood the task'.

We have organised the book in the following units.

In **Unit 1** we provide the justification for cooperative grouping from theory, research and the demands of the National Curriculum.
Unit 2 illustrates the different forms of grouping available and the design of tasks.
Unit 3 provides advice on choosing groups.
Unit 4 focuses on group management and training, including the creation of teacher time.
Unit 5 concentrates on the critical role of monitoring and assessment. And finally,
Unit 6 provides guidance on the specifics of setting up groupwork in the classroom.

We would like to stress that cooperative groupwork should be used as one strategy among other forms of classroom management, so that teachers achieve a balance between individualised tasks, group work and class activities.

How to use this book

The five sections of this book constitute a substantial course in groupwork. Each section provides a text together with written and discussion activities suitable for in-service or professsional studies courses.

The text may be read as a book in its own right; all the *activities* can be undertaken either individually or as a focus for a group.

The discussion activities are intended to be central to group meetings, though an individual reader will find the discussion questions useful as a prompt for reflection and planning.

The written activities are intended to be worked on individually but also lend themselves to group discussion when completed.

The practical activities included in the final section are designed for individual teachers to take into their own classroom.

The discussion and written activities associated with each of the six sections provide materials for a series of sessions lasting between 1 and 1½ hours. The practical classroom-based activities are appropriate for shorter periods, probably nearer to half an hour, but this is left entirely to the class teacher's discretion.

Although we encourage individuals to use this book, we believe that there is special value to be gained from a whole school policy for developing groupwork, when the shared practical activities will promote further discussion and experimentation.

The following symbols are used throughout the book to denote:

 quotations from published material

 activities

transcripts of children talking and feedback from teachers

WHY SHOULD CHILDREN WORK IN GROUPS?

INTRODUCTION TO GROUPWORK

The introduction of the National Curriculum has, not surprisingly, created genuine concerns in the minds of primary teachers. We know, from our own national surveys (Wragg, Bennett and Carré, 1989), that teachers are worried about their competence or confidence to teach such subjects as Science, Technology and Music, and about how they can possibly find the time for the continuous assessment and recording of each child's performance and progress across the curriculum. In addition, there is some anxiety about how best to satisfy statements of attainment in areas that have not previously been emphasised. Competencies and skills in collaborative endeavours and in oracy are two such areas.

Can these very real difficulties be overcome? We believe that there is a form of organisation – cooperative groupwork – that can substantially overcome the above concerns whilst at the same time holding out the promise of improved learning and social skills.

The reaction of some teachers to this suggestion is that they already do groupwork. So what's new? It is certainly true that most teachers have children seated in groups and talking in groups, but it is mistaken to think that this represents cooperative learning, as we shall see later when we consider some of the research evidence. In reality cooperative learning is something that few teachers achieve, as the delightfully named Schmuck (1985) argues:

> Why have we humans been so successful as a species? We are not strong like tigers, big like elephants, protectively coloured like lizards, or swift like gazelles. We are intelligent, but an intelligent human alone in the forest would not survive for long. What has really made us such successful animals is our ability to apply our intelligence to cooperating with others to accomplish group goals. From the primitive hunting group to the corporate boardroom, it is those of us who can solve problems while working with others who succeed. In fact, in modern society, cooperation in face-to-face groups is increasingly important. A successful scientist must be able to cooperate effectively with other scientists, with technicians, and with students. An executive must cooperate with other executives, salespersons, suppliers and superiors.
>
> Of course, each of those relationships also has competitive elements, but in all of them, if the participants cannot cooperate to achieve a common goal, all lose out. It is difficult to think of very many adult activities in which the ability to cooperate with others is not important.
>
> Because schools socialise children to assume adult roles, and because cooperation is so much a part of adult life, one might expect that cooperative activity would be emphasised. However, this is far from true. Among the prominent institutions of our society, the schools are least characterised by cooperative activity.

Although Schmuck is talking from an American perspective, it is the 'group-goals' about which he writes that will be central to our arguments. Yet how do we know that cooperative groupwork is not just another fad which will actually turn out either to increase demands on teachers, or be extremely difficult to implement in the busy primary classroom? Firstly (as we report in the next unit), there is a substantial body of theory and research to justify cooperative learning. In addition, we have been studying classroom grouping for more than eight years; and for two years we have collaborated with teachers to find out whether cooperative grouping really works and what difficulties, if any, they have had in setting it up.

For all these teachers, cooperative grouping in the form we describe through this workbook was entirely new, but without exception they have found it easier to implement than they imagined. Typical comments were 'I was pleasantly surprised at how easy the sessions were', and 'The children performed in a more business-like way than I'd expected'. Most of the teachers also commented on how much the children enjoyed such groupwork and how enthusiastic they were to continue to work in this way. One initially sceptical teacher said she 'was agreeably surprised to find that the children were in fact able to use each other and help each other more than I realised.'

You may, by this time, be asking, 'What does cooperative groupwork look like?' Essentially what we are attempting is to change typical classroom practice from children working *in* groups, to children working *as* groups, in other words, to move from children working on individual tasks in a group setting to their working on cooperative tasks. By this means, the quality of children's talk (and the underlying thought processes) should be enhanced and a corresponding improvement in the quality of their completed work should be seen.

The freeing of teacher time, which is a consequence of cooperative groupwork (as we will show in Unit 5), is also important, and here too the results have been encouraging. We know, from our own observations, that time was created in each classroom, and the teacher comments bear this out. 'Much more time is available to teach rather than to deal with many matters which can be peer assisted.' Another reinforced this, stating that 'It is a management method that really frees the teacher, and would enable her to carry out the profiling, observation and testing jobs.' So much time was freed in some classrooms that the teachers began to feel guilty at not being rushed off their feet – 'I found it very satisfying teaching in this way because the children were so involved in their work. It gave me a lot of free time . . . At times this made me feel that I was not doing my job.' Although several teachers had felt anxious at first about devolving responsibility to the groups, they in fact found there had been no need to worry about the lack of control over the whole class, and as teachers they became involved in other ways.

The extent and quality of children's involvement was commented on by all teachers who saw, for example 'a dramatic increase in the amount of discussion, suggestion, testing, inferring and drawing informed conclusions' and 'rich mathematical language.' They reported 'work that was more thorough and presented well' and children who were 'thinking and reflecting their views and not a teacher's.' One stated of a poetry activity: 'I was delighted that this whole assignment had developed the conditions for such high quality learning to take place.'

Low attainers particularly seemed to benefit and in some cases they 'now often sit with higher ability children who took them under their wing. On the other hand we have evidence to show how much high attainers gain from group work. The benefits to both low and high attainers are looked at in Unit 3.

Overall, the teachers with whom we have worked in the past, and those with whom we continue to work, are positive about the benefits of the approach, seeing it as beneficial to themselves in terms of releasing teacher time, and beneficial to children in terms of greater independence, greater cooperation and better quality work from both low and high attainers.

So, before we go any further, we would like you to consider your own practice and the reasons underlying it.

ACTIVITY 1

Answer the following questions in the space provided or, if you prefer, on a separate sheet. (Student teachers should answer the questions in relation to the class that they have current or most recent knowledge of).

1 INDIVIDUALISED WORK

If you provide individualised work for the children in your class:

i) For what proportion of the day do children work on individual tasks?

ii) What do you think are the main advantages and disadvantages of this as a way of managing learning?

2 GROUPWORK

If you group the children in your class

i) For what proportion of the day do children work *in groups* ie. seated together but working on individual tasks?

ii) What proportion of the day do they work *as groups* ie. seated together working on tasks that require a group outcome?

iii) How do you compose these groups; eg. what size are they? Are they based on age, sex, friendship, ability (ie. attainment) or any combination of these?

iv) What are the reasons for your choice of group composition?

v) Does the group composition change for different curriculum areas, and if it does, why is this so?

continued

3 i) What are the benefits (either for you or for the pupils) of children working in groups?

ii) Are there disadvantages to this way of working?

4 CLASS TEACHING

If you use whole class teaching for any lessons:

i) What proportion of the day is used for class teaching?

ii) What do you think are the main advantages and disadvantages of whole class teaching?

When you have completed your answers for questions 1 to 4, exchange them with a colleague, or colleagues, and discuss the differences which may be apparent. Can you justify your answers to the other's satisfaction?

Preparation for practical work in groups

In this review of your own practice and that of others, it is likely to show that you use a variety of different teaching strategies and have many different reasons for doing so. We do not suggest that any of these is wrong or inadequate, but that, despite very few teachers making use of truly cooperative groups, there are good reasons for their doing so.

We believe that cooperative grouping can be justified on at least four grounds:

1. It is necessary to meet particular attainment targets in the National Curriculum.
2. It can provide the time that teachers so critically need for assessing and recording in the classroom.
3. Current grouping practices may be improved by this means.
4. The research evidence shows the likelihood of clear improvements in pupils' social and intellectual development.

We now consider each of these points in turn.

COOPERATION AND ORACY IN THE NATIONAL CURRICULUM

In the National Curriculum for English, stress has been placed on the role of cooperation in Speaking and Listening. In meeting the attainment targets for collaboration pupils should be able, along with other skills, to:

Level 1 Speak freely, and listen, one-to-one to a peer.

Level 2 Present real or imaginary events in a connected narrative to a small group of peers.

Level 3 In a range of activities (including problem-solving), speak freely, and listen, to a small group of peers.

Level 4 Describe an event or experience to a group of peers, clearly, audibly and in detail. Give and receive precise instructions and follow them. Ask relevant questions with increasing confidence. Offer a reasoned explanation of how a task has been done or a problem has been solved. Take part effectively in a small group discussion and respond to others in the group.

Level 5 Speak freely and audibly to a large audience of peers and adults. Discuss and debate constructively, advocating and justifying a particular point of view. Contribute effectively to a small group discussion which aims to reach agreement on a given assignment.

One of the most valuable contributions of the National Curriculum English document is that it highlights the central role of talk in learning. This has been appreciated by both teachers and researchers for some considerable time. The Bullock Report (1975), for example, was a powerful advocate.

> We welcome the growth in interest in oral language in recent years, for we cannot emphasise too strongly our convictions of its importance in the education of the child . . . A priority objective for all schools is a commitment to the speech needs of their pupils and a serious study of the role of oral language in learning.

Some years later the Assessment of Performance Unit (APU) argued, on the basis of their evidence, that:

> The experience of expressing and shaping ideas through talk as well as writing, and of collaborating to discuss problems or topics, helps to develop a critical and exploratory attitude towards knowledge and concepts . . . It is likely that pupils' performance could be substantially improved if they were given regular opportunities in the classroom to use their speaking and listening skills over a range of purposes, in a relaxed atmosphere. (1986)

Similar views have been expressed in other influential reports such as the Cockroft Report on Mathematics (1982) and by recent HMI Surveys. For example, in their survey of primary maths they argued that

> Cooperative work was a strong and distinctive feature of the best mathematics work seen, with pupils seeking together a solution to an intellectual or practical problem. (HMI, 1989)

In the Science report they similarly stated:

> In much of the best work the children undertake investigations in small groups. This helps them to develop their ability to cooperate, to communicate, to negotiate and to respect each other's views. In working together they also learn to share ideas and teach skills to each other. (HMI, 1989)

These views have been derived from observations of practice but are supported by psychologists interested in children's learning.

For example Vygotsky (1962), a respected Russian psychologist, stresses the importance of the social situation in learning and argues 'What a child can do today in cooperation, tomorrow he will be able to do on his own.' For him, cooperatively achieved success is the foundation of learning and development irrespective of subject area. The foundation of that cooperatively achieved success is based on talk: talk is central to social development and to cognitive growth and the two are closely intertwined. In this book, our particular interest is in the way that groups allow children to give meaning to academic tasks; how discussing, describing, explaining and arguing allow pupils to develop their own meanings and how, in the words of Wells (1987): '. . . learning through talk – as in learning to talk – children are active constructors of their own knowledge.' For example, in discussion, children test out ideas; in explaining, children have to structure their knowledge and find words that will be understood by other children; in arguing, they have to make their own opinions known as well as justifying them.

In their journal, *Talk*, the National Oracy Project give a summary of the changes in practice with regard to language in schools. This summary is helpful in further drawing out the links between groupwork, talking and other uses of language. It also provides a useful rationale for parents who place greater value on reading and writing than on speaking and listening.

> Traditionally, perhaps still to many parents, the view of the school has been of the place where the chattering had to stop. The teacher talked, passing on the knowledge and information, and the children listened, soaking it up for future use. Written work and reading were individual, quiet activities, done by the child and checked by the teacher.

Nowadays, it is generally believed that:

. . . by talking, discussing, arguing, planning, describing, every day in school, children become better at doing those things, so that they have skills ready for the job interview, the work place – and for sorting out the situations that family life often throws up. They become better at chairing meetings, at summing up both sides of an argument, at absorbing evidence and forming hypotheses, at telling an effective story.

Speaking and listening, within a cooperative context, are abilities developed across the curriculum and in different contexts, as the planning diagram included in the National Curriculum Council advice (1989) shows. This is reproduced below and shows how planning concerns relate to programmes of study (POS) in English.

ACTIVITY 2

This section has stressed the inter-relatedness of cooperation and talk through such activities as discussing, arguing, explaining, etc. Consider your own classroom practice and identify those contexts which, in a typical week, allow children these opportunities.

TIME FOR ASSESSMENT

'In principle it would appear that the National Curriculum has a lot to offer. However, with the extra demands of record keeping, possibly testing and marking, it makes me wonder if we will have time enough to teach.'

This was a typical comment from a teacher in the national survey we carried out of over 900 teachers about their views on the implementation of the National Curriculum. When we asked which 'professional skills' they found most difficult in the classroom, seven in every ten teachers identified the diagnosis of children's learning difficulties; nearly two-thirds cited the continuous assessment of children's work and nearly one half said record keeping. (Wragg, Bennett and Carré, 1989).

Teachers' anxieties in these areas are easy to understand. It is becoming increasingly clear how important assessment is in relation to both teacher planning and pupil learning. As the Task Group on Assessment (TGAT) argued,

Assessment should be an integral part of the education process, continually providing both 'feedback' and 'feedforward'. It therefore needs to be incorporated systematically into teaching strategies and practices. (1988)

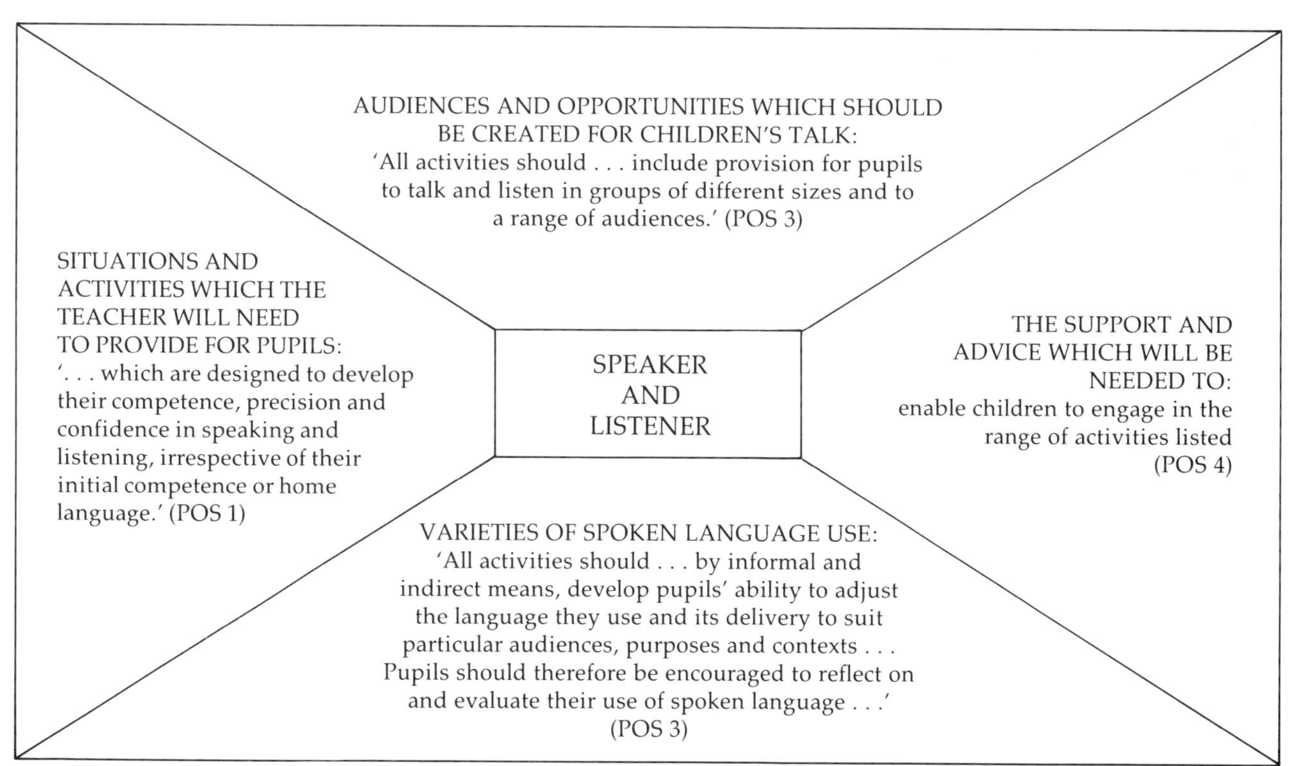

Speaking and listening: in relation to Programmes of Study in English

But systematic assessment, particularly the kind of diagnostic assessment that we would like to see, takes time (for further information on diagnosis, see *Assessment for Learning*, in this series). Marking a page of sums may be relatively speedy, but probing children's understanding of what they are doing takes considerably longer. Where is this time to come from, when there is an ever-increasing demand on teachers for continuous assessment and record keeping in relation to an ever-increasing number of attainment targets? Our evidence shows clearly that time can be created when teachers use cooperative groupwork, so long as they insist that children use their group for information and help. The teacher is then no longer seen as the fount of all knowledge, nor as the first port of call for low level requests for clarification and so on: 'Please Miss, do I need a margin?', 'Can I borrow a rubber?' or 'Could you spell "because"?' The group takes this responsibility. Our recent work with teachers shows that the number of pupil requests declines radically in such situations and the requests that are made are of a higher level and concerned with real difficulties in understanding. We consider this in greater detail in Unit 4.

CURRENT GROUPING PRACTICES

As we said in the introduction, teachers often respond to our call for more cooperative groupwork by saying that they already do it. Our answer would be – 'yes you probably do, but if you are a typical teacher your groupwork will rarely involve full cooperation.' Let's consider the evidence.

Research shows that most teachers seat their children in groups of between four and six pupils but the basis on which the groups are composed varies from free pupil choice to differentiation by ability. Grouping by ability appears to be the most common. Yet, whilst most children sit in groups, for most of their time they work as individuals on their own tasks.

The most extensive study of junior children (Galton, Simon and Croll 1980) tells a dismal story about grouping. Among the findings were the following: whilst in groups, the pupils on average spent two-thirds of the time working on their own, talking with no one; one-sixth of the time was spent relating to other pupils. However, most of this talk was not related to the task. Indeed, of the total time observed in groups only five per cent was spent talking with other pupils in relation to work. Further, most of the talk was directed to children of the same sex. Boys tended not to talk to girls and vice versa. Finally, it was exceptional to find a group working on a group task. *Only 10 per cent of all work observed in this study was cooperative groupwork.* In other words pupils work *in* groups, but not *as* groups.

A recent study on infant children (Bennett, Desforges, Cockburn and Wilkinson, 1984) presents a more optimistic picture with regard to the quantity of talk between children, but not with regard to the quality. Talk was mostly of a lower order, so for example, the amount of talk used in passing on knowledge or explanations was very low; in language work most of the requests were for spellings and the children did not seem clear about the teachers' expectations regarding cooperation.

The major weakness of current grouping practice seems to be that there is usually no specific demand on children to work together, and rarely is a group given the opportunity to work on a group task.

In diagrammatic terms we can conceive typical group practice as either 1 or 2 below.

1 Working individually on *different tasks* for individual products

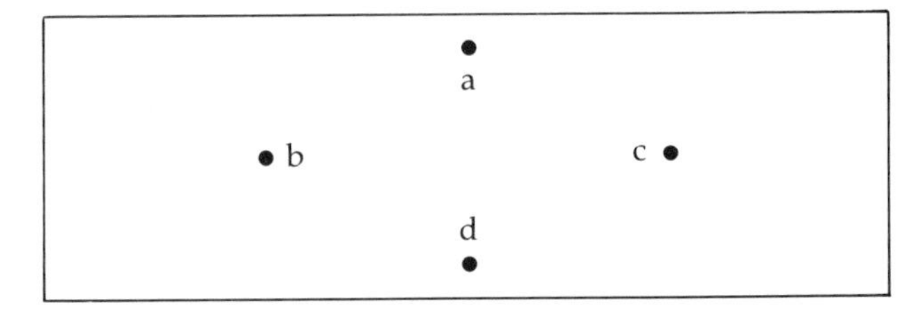

2 Working individually on *identical tasks* for individual products

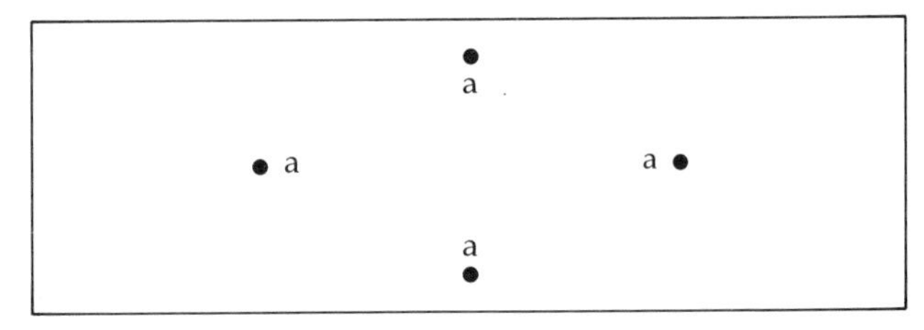

• = children
a, b, etc = tasks

1 This is typical in maths where children are working on a structured scheme but are each at different stages. This even occurs when children sit in homogeneous ability groups. So each of the children works on different, i.e. individual, tasks, each aiming for an individual end product.

2 This is more common in writing where the teacher's request is often for a class task, e.g. the writing of a story. In this case all the children are engaged on identical work, but there is no demand for cooperation.

What seems to have happened in practice is that teachers have taken on board the views of the Plowden Report (1967) on having children work in groups, but have preferred to retain individualisation rather than cooperation in that context. As one educationalist wrote:

> Grouping thus emerges as an organisational device rather than as a means of promoting more effective learning, or perhaps exists for no reason other than that fashion and ideology dictate it. (Alexander, 1984)

The lack of demand for cooperation in typical classroom groups shows itself in the quality of the talk in which children engage. In our infant study referred to above, children talked a great deal about how much work each had done, about procedures for using materials, about how clever, or otherwise they were, and about what they would do at playtime, after school or at the weekend. What tended not to be included in their conversations were explaining, demonstrating, giving, discussing, decision-making, and the like. In other words, although a good deal of their talk was task-related, it was rarely task-enhancing; that is, it did not further the successful completion of their work.

It was also clear from reading the transcripts that children were sometimes confused about what was allowed. On the one hand they were working in a group of children, but on the other the teacher would want them to work by themselves. The purposes of grouping, or children talking, seems unclear in such circumstances.

'You're not allowed to let people help you. Don't help her, Stuart.'

'Well, you have to go and learn yourself . . . so you'll have to do it yourself, Hayley.'

RESEARCH EVIDENCE ON THE EFFECTIVENESS OF COOPERATIVE GROUPWORK

Cooperative groupwork can also be justified on the grounds of research evidence. Much of this research has emanated from the United States. Until recently, the British interest in cooperative groupwork has been based more on assertion than research, but current work, including our own, should provide important evidence of its benefits. The kinds of assertion made can be seen both in reports of Committees of Enquiry, such as the Bullock Report (1975), and in many HMI reports. A few examples will suffice. Bullock, not surprisingly, focused on the development of language in groups.

> When the children bring language to bear on a problem within a small group their talk is often tentative, discursive, implicit and uncertain of direction . . . the intimacy of the context allows this to happen without any sense of strain. In an atmosphere of tolerance, of hesitant formulation and of co-operative effort the children can 'stretch' their language to accommodate their own second thoughts and the opinions of others. They can float their notions without fear of having them dismissed.(para. 10.12)

Similarly, the 1978 Primary School Survey claimed that,

> . . . children of all ages, and especially young children, benefit from being given opportunities for discussion in small groups since it is easier for each to make a contribution and to feel an essential member of the group. More opportunities for small group discussion might usefully be arranged in the work of the schools.

Later the 8-12 Middle School Survey (1985) suggested that in different situations children '. . . need to be given more opportunities to pose questions, to predict and to speculate'.

As we saw earlier, the most recent HMI report on Mathematics (1989) was worded even more strongly:

> Cooperative work was a strong and distinctive feature of the best mathematics work seen, with pupils seeking together a solution to an intellectual or practical problem.

In the United States, the research findings show that cooperative learning promotes:

- higher achievement
- higher self esteem
- greater inter-personal attraction and more positive relationships between pupils irrespective of sex, race or handicap (cf Slavin, 1983; Johnson and Johnson, 1975).

Evidence is now beginning to accumulate in Britain which is supportive of the above findings.

In our recent work, for example, we have demonstrated a highly significant increase in the amount of task related talk in cooperative, as opposed to typical, groups.

	COOPERATIVE GROUPWORK (Bennett and Dunne 1989)	INDIVIDUALISED WORK IN GROUPS (Bennett et al 1984)
MATHS	89%	63%
LANGUAGE	86%	70%
TOTAL	88%	

Not only did task related talk increase by 22% overall (the increase being consistent in both maths and language tasks), but, more importantly, the nature of the task changed. Rather than evidence of a good deal of self interest when children worked in an individual situation, cooperative groupwork led to real collaboration, the sharing of ideas and knowledge, the solving of problems together and real concern for the progress of the group as a whole.

Finally, it depends on what you want to call evidence. The 'evidence' we present in the introduction from the teachers who have implemented some form of cooperative groupwork would indicate clearly that, as far as they are concerned, it works on all counts.

a ACTIVITY 3

Discuss the following questions:

The evidence would indicate that typical grouping practice, i.e. children working *in* groups not *as* groups, has some unfortunate consequences.

1 From reading the text and from your own experience, consider what these consequences are and why you think they occur.
2 How, from the evidence presented, and from your own knowledge of children, do you think cooperative grouping could help to overcome these problems?

Having looked at the justification and evidence for cooperative groupwork, we now consider different approaches to planning and preparation.

TYPES OF COOPERATIVE GROUPWORK

THE STRUCTURE OF THE TASK

Very little has been written about the kinds of task that are most appropriate for cooperative groupwork. It has been suggested that groupwork might be approached in stages, leading gradually from simple, brief activities with a narrow focus (for example, word games and puzzles) to more generalised problem-solving activities. It is also stressed by both American and British writers that cooperative groupwork need in no way distort the normal school curriculum, but is a way of working within it.

The tasks discussed in this book have all been designed by teachers with the National Curriculum in mind. They should provide ideas for the reader, to use and adapt as appropriate to their classroom situation. They also demonstrate the ways in which tasks set for pupils working as individuals can be translated into a cooperative group activity. For some tasks, it is the demand for sharing ideas, for solving a problem or for understanding the activity that makes it appropriate to groupwork; for other tasks it is the need to produce a group end product rather than a series of individual ones.

This section on the structure of the task will enlarge on these issues.

It seems common sense that certain types of class management and certain types of task are more likely to promote cooperation than others. Clearly, cooperation is likely to be limited when children work at individualised workschemes, and this is in part because pupils who are helping others will be taken away from their own tasks. However, when pupils are asked for a joint outcome or product (for example, when they work together to solve a problem, to make something or for a discussion), cooperation is essential to fulfil the demands of the task.

Below, we outline three possible models for types of task; the demands for cooperation are slightly different in each one.

1 Working individually on *identical tasks* for individual products

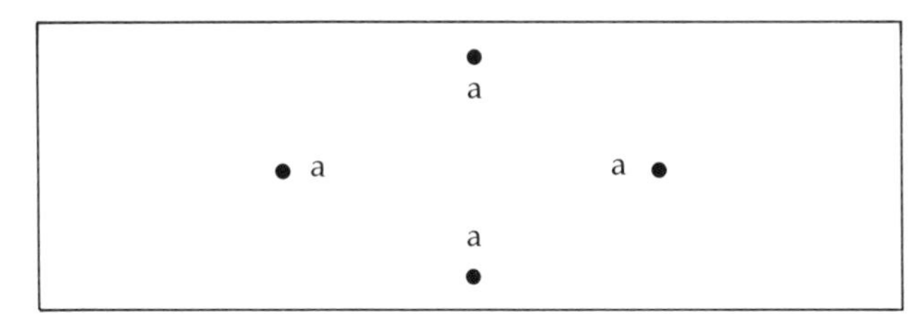

• = children
a = tasks

On the surface, this model does not look like a cooperative group structure, for individuals are asked to provide individual products. We did in fact present this same model in the previous unit when considering children working individually in groups. Yet, when children in a group are working on *the same task* it is possible for them to share the experience and contribute to each other's interest, motivation or understanding. Their talk may influence each other's actions, ideas and the quality of the end product. But it is unlikely that this will occur unless the teacher specifically demands and encourages this kind of behaviour. Since children are asked for individual products, the task does not in itself demand cooperation.

Any activity in the classroom can be set up in this way, for example, story writing, practical maths work and so on.

Individual boats are made, but watching and talking in the group context may be very important when all children tackle the same task.

2 Working individually on 'jigsaw' elements for a joint outcome

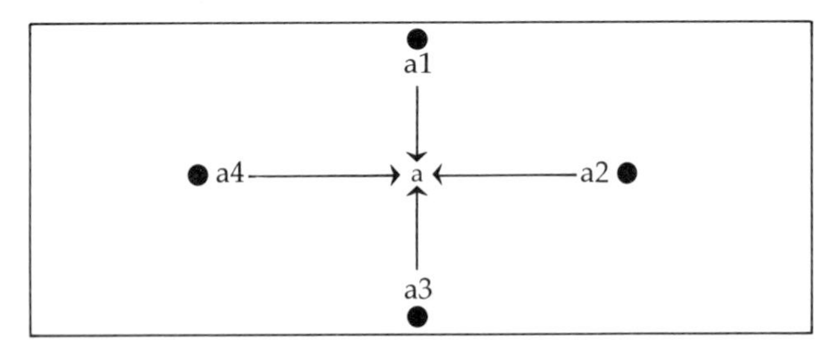

In this kind of task, there are as many elements to the task as there are group members. Each child works on one element and the task is divided in such a way that the group outcome cannot be achieved until every group member has successfully completed their piece of work. At this point the 'jigsaw' can be fitted together. Cooperation is thus built into the task structure, as indeed is individual accountability. It is difficult in this type of group task for a child to sit back and let others do all the work, especially since group members are likely to ensure that everyone pulls their weight.

Examples of such tasks would be the production of a group story or newspaper, or the making of a 'set' of objects in a practical maths activity.

3 Working jointly on one task for a joint outcome (or discussion)

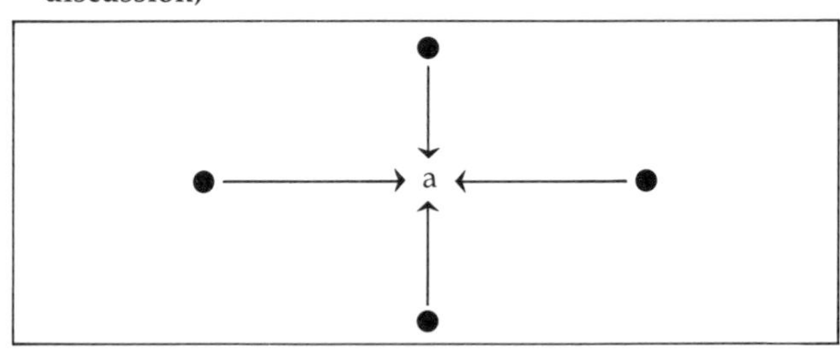

A joint task: all children work together to complete the group worksheet.

For this type of task, children will need to work cooperatively since only one product will be required of the group. Activities will therefore have to be coordinated and it is possible that a group leader will emerge, or could be selected, in order to create the necessary organisation. Each individual's work will have an impact on the group product but will be worthless until it becomes part of that product.

Examples can be seen in problem solving in technology and construction activities (say, when a whole group is making a single cart) or in discussion tasks. Although collaborative endeavour is necessary for the group to succeed, it is less easy to ascertain exactly what each group member has contributed and individual accountability is therefore lower.

These three models demonstrate that cooperative groupwork is not a single, specific form of classroom organisation but encompasses different approaches with children working in different ways. The main objective is always, however, that children should work cooperatively together.

ACTIVITY 4

To familiarise yourself with these models, consider the following questions. It may be useful to write notes or draw representations of your own.

1 What are the main similarities and differences between these three models?

2 Do you have a preference at this stage? If so, which is it? Why do you prefer it?

CHOICE OF TASKS AND TYPE OF TALK – EXAMPLES FROM MATHS AND TECHNOLOGY

'It seems that choosing the task is probably the most important aspect of group work.' This feeling is one shared by many teachers.

We have just looked at three possible models for cooperative tasks. Now we discuss how the choice of a task to fit each one of these models is likely to have a different impact on the ways in which children work and talk. Firstly, we look at three lessons with pupils working at practical activities for maths or technology. Each model for groupwork is considered in turn.

1 Working individually on identical tasks for individual products

In the task shown below, the four children are making cuboids from card for a maths task. The group of seven and eight year olds has been asked to cooperate, as the extracts of talk will show. Although each child is working individually, the context of the group is considered to be important. The conversation is slightly difficult to follow since the children are each reporting their own progress to the others.

Teacher:	Remember you're working as a group, not on your own. Help each other.
Peter:	Oh, cooey, I've done it wrong.
Richard:	Brill, finished. Do you think that's a perfect . . .?
Tania:	I'm going to make another one because I did that one wrong. It won't stick up like that. Something's wrong there.
Susan:	Oh, I have to do this again, it's rubbish. Tania, I have to do this again cos it's rubbish, isn't it?
Peter:	I've finished nearly – ha, ha.
Teacher:	Well you must ask the rest of your group, because you might not have done. I didn't hear you asking anyone.
Richard:	I asked Tania – the nearest.

It can be seen here that, although the task itself does not demand cooperation, the teacher wants the children to work together, to help each other, to be aware of what others are doing and how they are working. The group (rather than the individual) is given responsibility for the quality of each end product and the pupils need therefore to turn to each other to check for correctness. Although the teacher controls this process at the beginning of the lesson, she quickly moves away and the children clearly show immediate concern for one another and the quality of the work.

Tania:	It doesn't matter, just fold it again right. It doesn't matter, it doesn't matter . . . you don't have to start again.
Susan:	I gotta do it again.
Peter:	There is something wrong with it.
Tania:	Let's make sure, where's yours?
Susan:	There's something wrong with it.
Richard:	Yeah there is . . . there must be. (Pause)
Richard:	Brill . . . it's getting more and more good
Susan:	Is that correct Tania?
Tania:	Mmmmm . . . Yep.

ACTIVITY 5

Discuss the following questions:

1 Is there any evidence that the teacher's demands are being heeded?
2 To what extent are these children controlling the quality of their group's work, and how do they do this?
3 Do you think that this type of talk between children is of positive benefit to them? If so, can you say why? If not, give your reasons.

2 Working individually on 'jigsaw' elements for a joint outcome

We now look at children working on an activity similar to that of the previously described lesson. However, the need to cooperate is built into the task.

Four six year old children work on the same task in a randomly selected group. They have been shown and have practised one example of a specific method for making an open-topped box using square paper measuring 10 cm by 10 cm. They have now been asked to work as a group to find out how many different boxes can be made from that same-sized piece of paper. In order to meet the task demand, children have to work cooperatively but each must produce his or her own different-sized box.

(James is asking Natalie how to count the squares to be cut out for the corners).

James: Do you just go up to 2?
Natalie: One, two, one, two, one, two (demonstrates where to cut).
James: I'm doing a 4 by 4 (ie. 4 by 4 squares cut from each corner).
Paul: I'm doing 11 by 11 (the group laughs, presumably since they are aware that this is impossible).
Lucy: I'm doing 3 by 3.
James: I'm doing 4 by 4.
Paul: I'm cutting out one square from each corner.
Natalie: One square?
Paul: Yeah (laughs).
(There is now a period in which they can all be heard counting to themselves.)
Lucy: I'm doing a 3 by 3 which leaves 4 in the middle.
James: Mine only leaves 2 in the middle.
Lucy: Two in the middle?
James: Yeah (laughs) Look!
Lucy: 5 by 5.
James: (laughs) That's not going to get anywhere!
James: }
Lucy: } (counting together) 1,2,3,4,5; 1,2,3,4,5; 1,2,3,4,5; 1,2,3,4,5.
Natalie: That's a 10 by 10 now. . .I mean . . .
(James cuts, counting as he goes)
James: I think she won't be able to make one out of 5 by 5 (group laughter). (James holds up a 5 by 5 square to show his 10 by 10 square is now cut into four separate pieces.)
You can make one out of 4 by 4 but you can't make one out of 5 by 5.

ACTIVITY 6

Discuss the following questions:

1 What is the impact of the task structure on the children's talk and ways of working?
2 What differences might there be between the kind of talk above and that where:
   a) All children are working on individual and different tasks.
   b) Children are working on the same task but are not specifically asked to cooperate.

3 Working jointly on one task for a joint outcome

When a task demands only one artefact to be produced by the whole group, cooperation is essential.

The following snippets of talk illustrate some of the difficulties experienced by children aged seven to eight negotiating a group task. These pupils are building a small cart together. (Paul starts in a fairly negative manner.)

Paul: I don't know what to do.
(He quickly rephrases his question and becomes interested in the task.)
Paul: What can I do? I've got the sticking bit . . . I've got the wood sticking, I've got this one . . . no I've got this one . . . what shall I stick? .. one of those and a pencil?
(Unfortunately he is rebuffed.)
Jane: Sorry, Paul, Stacey's doing it. Put it on this one for her.
Because you're not my best friend, wait a minute. There's plenty of sawing, look, these and these.
(Gradually he gains responses, for example):
Paul: I'm not doing anything . . . What shall I do?
Stacey: See if you can hold it there.
(Jane then organises the situation to give each group member a chance to saw.)
Jane: Paul and Hayley can do the next bit of sawing.

ACTIVITY 7

1 Do you think these children are used to working together? How well do they cooperate?
2 What sort of instruction might a teacher give to make children more aware of each other's needs?
3 In what ways are the children's negotiations important to their learning/to the completion of the task?

CHOICE OF TASKS AND TYPE OF TALK – EXAMPLES FROM LANGUAGE WORK

The tasks we have presented to you so far have been either Maths or Technology activities. Now we look at some language tasks.

A

Four children aged eleven are discussing a story they have read.

Sophie: The ending was hopeless.
Holly: Was it? Do you think it was?
Luke: I liked the ending.
Sophie: It was too soppy though.
Luke: Too soppy?
Neil: Well I like it when they die at endings. It makes it a lot more funnier. It's a lot more good.
Holly: Well that's very nice isn't it? (sarcastically!)
Neil: Its a lot more good – like – like – if I wrote a story I'd go 'as he swings his head with his sword' and stop the book there and they'd want to buy the next book wouldn't they?
Holly: No, probably wouldn't – because not many people like animals being killed.
Neil: They would.

ACTIVITY 8

Discuss the following questions:

1 To what extent are these children challenging each other's ideas?
2 Do the children *all* justify their own opinions? In what ways?
3 Which model of task structure does this task best fit?

B

Nine and ten year olds are given a long poem which is read both with the teacher and by the group. The children are asked to draw individual posters to illustrate the poem and told also that they may be challenged about its meaning. Each drawing needs to reflect the description and sense of the poem, and the children thus search for meaning as this becomes important to their illustration:

Whole group discussion

Mary Anne: No I'm not. I'm sitting him down with his hands over his face crying. He's an old man isn't he?
Samantha: I dunno. Yes I think . . . Does it say old? Does it say man?
Mary Anne: An old . . . yeah . . . It says 'the old King of the Makers'.
Samantha: If it says 'King' it must be a man.

They also need to know the meaning of individual words:

Matthew: . . . clayman. What's a clayman?
Mary Anne: How the hell should I know what a clayman is . . . A clayman is, a clayman is a clayman.
Matthew: No but you wouldn't find a clayman in the jungle.
Samantha: The cayman not a clayman.
Mary Anne: How should I know what a cayman is?
Matthew: Well go up and ask.

ACTIVITY 9

Discuss the following questions:

1 Which model of task structure does this task best fit?
2 In what ways are the children learning from each other (in so far as you can hypothesise from a small extract of talk)?
3 Do you think that the process of collaborative meaning making is important? Why?

C

A group of three six and seven year olds are discussing a problem: which choice – of a card, a cup of tea in bed, or a bunch of flowers – would be the best way to surprise Mum Cook on her birthday? The children enter into this hypothetical situation instantly, listening and replying to each other, making decisions, justifying their responses:

Andrew: Yes, but if we choose the flowers one she can put them in a vase.
Louise: Yes, but they'll die so she won't keep them for very long.
Andrew: She will because . . .
Louise: They could be, they could be, those paper flowers couldn't they . . . because they last a long time.

Then:

Louise: I think the card.
Andrew: Yeah the card.
Louise: Because Mum can keep it for ages, she could always keep it forever . . ... If we have a cup of tea Mum will drink it all.
Andrew: No she won't, she'll spill it.
Louise: In bed, she might spill the milk when she's pouring it in for her breakfast, so we'll have the card.
Donna: Yes.
Louise: Because, because, when the flowers are in the vase they could knock the vase over and the water would go over.

ACTIVITY 10

Discuss the following questions:

1 We feel that this is a highly appropriate activity for developing talk between six to seven year olds. Do you agree and can you say why or why not?
2 Do the children discuss each alternative? Is it important that they should do so?
3 In what ways do these children justify their own choices?
4 Do you feel concerned at the lack of participation by Donna? Can you say why or why not?
5 How would you respond to the children if you overheard this conversation?
6 If you teach older children, discuss possibilities for a similar problem solving task with a content appropriate to your particular age-group.

ACTIVITY 11

Making use of all the extracts of talk in this section, make notes on the major differences between the type of talk emerging from Maths/Technology tasks and Language tasks.

Note that the former tasks are all practical and therefore involve manipulation of materials, whereas the latter involve talk, discussion and decision-making unrelated to action.

TALK IN GROUPS WHERE CHILDREN ARE NOT REQUIRED TO WORK COOPERATIVELY

Having looked at the kind of talk emerging from cooperative work, it is interesting to compare it with talk from groups in which children are seated together but work individually.

1 Children's perceptions of how they should work

Read these three extracts and then discuss the questions below.

i) *Lisa:* A person who explores is a . . . Hey, this is easy.
Amanda: I know it is.
Lisa: A person who explores is an explorer.
Amanda: You heard my writing.
Lisa: What? I never copied.
Amanda: Well you heard what I said then.
Lisa: I never.
Amanda: I know that one.
Lisa: Tell me how to spell it. I don't know how. Soldier.
Amanda: Look in the dictionary.

ii) Members of the group insist . . .
'you're not allowed to let people help you. Don't help her Stuart', and,
'Well you have to go and learn yourself . . . so you'll have to do it yourself Hayley.'

iii) Suzanne seems to have been puzzling over a sum for several minutes:
Suzanne: I don't understand this one.
Lisa: Don't you? What is it?
Suzanne: That one. I leave home at 20 past 8.
Lisa: I leave home at 20 past 8 and I get to school at . . . Oh I don't know. You have to work it out.
Suzanne: I know I'm going to work it. But . . .

Some while later, Suzanne goes to the teacher.

If the aim is individualised work, what is the purpose of talking?

ACTIVITY 12

Discuss the following:

1 What sort of messages have these children received from their teachers about copying?
2 When does helping become copying? Can this be avoided?
3 To what extent do you think individualised work leads to the type of talk above?
4 What strategies would you use to clarify for children what is appropriate 'helping' behaviour and when it should be used?

2 Status

Katy: Hey, these are good. This card, card five is good, isn't it?
Fiona: Why?
Katy: Oh, they're easy sums.
Fiona: I like hard sums. Do you like easy ones best?

Katy does not answer, but reads out her sum. Then:

Katy: These are easier than the others. Hey Fiona, these sums are easier than the others.

Fiona has been talking to Amanda who has come back to the table, but replies:

Fiona: They're not when you get onto the black ones.

Katy: Why? Are those hard, the black ones?
Amanda: I'm on card twenty two now.
Katy: Twenty two. Oh Amanda. I got really muddled up. Look.
Amanda: On twenty two?
Fiona: I never, it's easy.

ACTIVITY 13

Discuss the following questions:

1 What are the children learning from one another?
2 In what ways could their talk further social development? Does it do so?
3 Why do you think these children are so concerned with their status?
4 To what extent are these children interested in their own learning, or merely with progress through a workscheme?

Unit 3

CHOOSING GROUPS

The National Curriculum makes it clear that teachers should set up different groups for different tasks and purposes.

The kind of groupwork discussed throughout this book lends itself best to situations where all groups work on the same task at the same time. However, we realise that this may not necessarily be possible or acceptable; for example, at times, and for certain kinds of activity, resources will be limited so that groups working on different tasks might be more appropriate. We have found, however, that when all groups work on the same task, the burden on teachers is often eased. It does not seem to create organisational problems. The use of team-teaching, or helpers and parents, may often allow for better management of groups in the classroom, but the aim of this book is to suggest alternative ways by which teachers can cope more easily with the many demands and pressures of classroom life. We hope that by using cooperative groupwork they will feel encouraged to allow children to take on more responsibility for their own work and the management of their own groups.

Our concern in this unit is to try to shed some light on the factors that teachers ought to take into account when setting up groups for cooperative work. These factors include group size and group composition.

ATTAINMENT MIX

As we indicated earlier, teachers vary in the manner in which they compose their groups. Many prefer ability (more properly, attainment) groups, but many do not, preferring mixed ability, friendship or interest groupings. Others use all these forms at one time or another for different tasks and subjects. Given this variation in practice, it is perhaps surprising that there is very little research on the effects of such variations, either on what happens in the group, or on the quality of what the group members produce.

Cooperative groupwork in science: fair testing of materials

Nevertheless some researchers (e.g. Bennett and Cass, 1988) have addressed teachers' perennial worries like 'Is ability grouping as effective for low attainers as high attainers?' and 'Do high attainers suffer in mixed ability groups?'

The short answer to both of these questions would seem to be 'no'. Groups composed entirely of high attainers perform very well, as you would expect. But groups of low attainers generally do very badly, their levels of knowledge and understanding being insufficient to provide each other with support. In our most recent work with teachers, very few of them allowed their children to work in groups of low attainers. When this did occur, the teacher was inevitably drawn towards these groups. This seemed to be mainly because of a lack of understanding of the task – even combined group efforts failed to sort out problems. In addition to this, low-attaining pupils were not drawn into the task in the same way as when working in a mixed-ability group; they seemed less able to share knowledge and communicate usefully and showed less skill in allowing, or encouraging, the group to work together.

One teacher describes how a group of low

attainers broke into sub-groups, working separately with little interaction, and how for a maths task they produced three separate graphs rather than one group presentation. She observes:

'As no-one had taken the role of leader or was acting as a peer tutor these problems were not overcome without teacher intervention. When the other members of the group were asked by the teacher to help Wendy and Michelle, they were willing and able to do so but there had been no previous assistance offered. Michelle and Wendy are both introverted pupils and they had not discussed their work within the group. Studies in America by Webb (1982) have shown that introverted pupils are less likely to receive explanations in response to errors than extroverted pupils, and there is evidence here of this happening. Overall there was little explaining done, a low level of instructional talk and infrequent suggestions so that the pupils gained very little academically from each other. It would appear the reasons for this are as Webb, and Bennett and Cass, have concluded, 'the students probably do not have enough skills or knowledge of the subject matter to give effective explanation . . .

The question could be asked whether the task was too difficult or unstructured for members of this group. However, I do not consider that it was, as when I encouraged group cooperation the information that Michelle and Wendy needed was provided by other members of the group. The weakness appeared to be within the group structure rather than within the task.'

Two of the boys in this group failed to complete their graphs and a group summary of the task was not attempted, whereas low-attainers in mixed-ability groups were enabled to work successfully by interacting with more able peers. Another teacher describes a similar situation, concluding:

'The low attaining group remained on task much more than was expected but produced little. The work was of poor quality with multiple errors due to the poor leadership within the group, lack of planning, lack of accurate assistance with low level requests, etc'.

We would not want to state categorically that low attaining children should never be allowed to work together, for there may well be a time and a purpose for this; but teachers should be aware that if groups of this type are set up, they must be prepared to provide considerable time and support to the lower attaining children.

Training in how to be effective in groupwork may also enable low attainers to operate more usefully, and this is considered in Unit 4. It is certainly true from our observations that low attaining children can be capable of skilful group leadership, given appropriate circumstances.

High attainers not only do well in high ability groups, they do well in whichever kind of group they find themselves. They are of particular value in mixed ability groups where they are able to support their lower attaining classmates with inputs of knowledge, as well as suggestions and explanations.

There seems no doubt that the high attaining children are often involved in all kinds of organising activities within their groups, both in terms of the cooperative demands of the tasks and the cognitive content. We can see this most clearly by considering 'real' children doing 'real' classroom tasks.

Thomas

Thomas is an interesting example of a ten year old who not only takes on the role of group leader, but also demonstrates skill in the way he enables and encourages others to work, thereby raising the standards of the whole group.

Five children in a mixed ability group have been collecting data during a class survey of cars. Their teacher reports:

'At the beginning of the lesson on the second day the groups had to decide upon different mathematical ways of showing their findings. In this group, Thomas ensured that a number of different methods were used. After finding out from Carley and Vanessa that they wanted to draw a bar graph he then told David and Nathan that they could do a pie-chart. The two boys readily agreed to this although it is unlikely that they would have been able to construct a pie-chart without help. Thomas gave Andrew the chance to choose and agreed to his suggestion of percentages but then added "If we do a line graph as well as percentages it'll make it better." Thus, in this group, four different methods of showing the pupils' findings were being used.

As the lesson progressed, the role of peer tutor, which Thomas had taken upon himself, became more marked as the following conversation between him and Carley illustrates:

Thomas: *(to Carley)*	How many colours have you got? You've got 1, 2, 3 . . . 9, 10. So if you write the colours along the bottom, and the numbers like 1, 1, 1. No, no, like 0, 5, 10, 15, 20 like that up the side. No, maybe less.
Carley:	Do we have to do it in 2's then?
Thomas:	Yes . . . in 4's might be better.
Carley:	4, 8 . . .
Thomas:	No, in 2's probably as it only goes up to 40.
Carley:	Oh, yes.
Thomas:	OK, right that will best. So you've got that. Just write the colours, there's 1, 2, 3 . . . 9 colours.

'Thomas planned the best way of drawing the graph as if it had been his own piece of work. Whilst he asked questions of Carley – "How many colours have you got?", he answered the question by counting the colours himself. Carley and Vanessa had not asked for assistance from Thomas and in fact, drawing a bar graph was a familiar task for them so that they could almost certainly have done this without help. The fact that Carley suggested doing it in 2's showed that she understood the idea of appropriate scale in graph work. However, the girls appeared to be happy to accept Thomas' advice and were content after this conversation to draw the graph as Thomas had suggested. In a similar way, Thomas supervised the making of a pie-chart by Nathan and David, even suggesting that they could "go outside and spot one more manual (gearbox)" in order to bring the number of cars they counted to 40 so that it would be easier to divide the pie-chart. (This is a good example of pupils using adaptive learning strategies in order to make the task easier to accomplish.) At the same time he was leading Andrew in their own task of producing a line graph and giving the percentages for cars from different countries of manufacture. When anyone in the group was having a problem, either in interpreting their information or in deciding how to present their findings, Thomas offered assistance. It appeared that he was able to do his own element of the task at the same time as listening to and helping the other members of the group. Whilst the pupils were working on different elements of the task they were held together as a group by the overview of Thomas.'

Although the members worked in sub-groups, there was interaction between Thomas and all the members of the group whilst they were working and this talk was all on the task. The group talked through the stages of the task, including the summary and prediction. It is clear from the extract of talk presented next, that if the group had consisted of only the less able members they would not have had sufficient knowledge to attempt either the summary or the prediction.

The following activity allows you to investigate the ways in which Thomas manages the group in this regard.

ACTIVITY 14

Thomas is involved in many kinds of talk during the extract of talk opposite. For example, he *questions*, he *allocates* work, he *summarises* arrangements. Firstly, read the extract through and then, in the box provided alongside, find words to describe each of Thomas's talk activities, following the examples given.

Then discuss these questions:

1 The words you have just provided may help you to consider the skills that Thomas will be developing as a group leader. How important are such skills?
2 In what ways do the rest of group react and respond to him?
3 What do you think Thomas learned?
4 To what extent do you think Thomas may have had an impact on the other children's learning?
5 To what extent might Thomas be considered over-dominant?

Thomas's talk activities

Thomas:	Now, the summary and the prediction. So how do you reckon we should write the summary?	*checks* the task *questions* the group
Nathan:	I don't know.	
David:	Nathan doesn't know.	
Vanessa:	Nor does David.	
Thomas:	Come on, think. OK, get Painer [ie. Andrew] to do it, alright.	
Andrew:	What?	
David:	What are you going to do Painer?	
Andrew:	I don't know.	
Thomas:	OK, you can do that Carley.	
Carley:	Eh?	
Thomas:	The summary of what we've learned.	
Carley:	We've learnt about cars.	
Thomas:	No, no, you've got to work out from what you get.	
David:	If we collect all our information together we could say how many red automatic cars there are and how many red manual cars there were.	
Carley:	Yes.	
Thomas:	On average from the number of cars we predicted we'll take the smallest number of cars found.	
Carley:	Right, yes.	
Thomas:	We can try it. (To Carley) If you do the summary. If Carley writes the summary from the information that we all give her. What about the prediction? What do you see as the prediction? What does she (the teacher) mean by prediction?	
Nathan:	A guess?	
Thomas:	A guess of what?	
Nathan:	Let's go a bit further than a guess. Is that what it means – let's go a bit further than a guess?	
Vanessa:	An estimate.	
Thomas:	Yes. We'll do the prediction after the summary.	

The teacher's comment is that:

'Without Thomas' guidance it seems very unlikely that anyone would have volunteered to write either the summary or the prediction or that the other group members would have known what was involved in doing these.'

GIRLS AND BOYS

There is a clear, and interesting, developmental trend in the relationships between girls and boys in primary schools. At the infant level girls and boys tend to relate happily together, but as they progress through the junior years there is an increasing tendency to mix and to talk with members of their own sex. Some studies have found that boys complain because girls just sit and say nothing, whereas girls argue that boys are so competitive and domineering that they are not encouraged to become involved.

The dilemma for the teacher is both a moral and an organisational one – should boys and girls be grouped together as a matter of principle to fulfil both social and academic goals, even if the children wish otherwise? Our own belief is that they should, at least some of the time, but this is an issue which each teacher must resolve to their own satisfaction.

As yet we have insufficient evidence to know whether single sex or mixed sex groups work better.

CHILDREN'S PERSONALITY

There are other important factors to consider when deciding on group composition. The quotes from teachers below illuminate these, as they explain how they choose their groups.

Teacher A
'I decided to mix boys and girls in the groups . . .
I decided to mix Junior with Top Infants, and Top Infants with Middle Infants, otherwise the age range might be too wide . . .
I had to consider the children's personalities together with age and ability.
Several of the Junior children were quite shy, while there were a number of children with assertive personalities . . .'

Teacher B
'I always tended to group children by ability, which usually leaves a group of low achievers who seem to demand a disproportionate amount of my time. For this particular study I made up heterogeneous groups with a low and a high achiever in each group and I also tried to ensure that there was a child in each group who could think 'creatively', someone who might be able to provide ideas.'

Teacher C
'I have become very aware in the course of my investigations that the dynamics of groups plays a major role in their effectiveness. It is not just a case of mixed ability, homogeneous or heterogeneous groupings. The personalities of the children involved, the activities they are given to do, even the time of day, have their effect on how the group operates . . . much thought needs to be given when organising groups. That the teacher needs to know the children's abilities very well, subject by subject, as a high performer in maths may not be so in language. It also points to the usefulness of grouping to split up children of similar ability who may be in friendship groups and would not normally choose to work with different ability children. The children obviously prefer to work in friendship groups, but many respond well to being 'arranged' into different groups.'

It is clear from these descriptions that teachers are very sophisticated in the range of criteria they use, stressing particularly children's personality traits. It is not easy to generalise about the effect of these, and decisions will depend on the teacher's assessment of the nature of interactions between the particular children in their class.

GROUP SIZE

In Britain the majority of teachers tend to set up groups of between four and six children. This pattern no doubt reflects teachers' attempts at making the best of space and furnishing constraints and curriculum resources. Less recognised, perhaps, is that group size effects the opportunity for, and the nature of, children's interactions, by determining the number of lines of communication.

If the research evidence is to be believed, then groups of four are the optimal size. One study concluded:

Teams of four are ideal. A team of three is often a dyad and an outsider; in a team of three there are three possible lines of communication; in a team of four there are six. Doubling the lines of communication increases learning potential . . . Teams of five often leave an odd man out and leave less time for individual participation. (Kagan, 1988)

A group of five can often break down into a pair and a trio.

As a general rule groups of three or four are preferable to larger groups. Our experience is that groups of five or six tend to break down in practice into pairs and trios. Although we have not carried out research on pairs of children working together, there is substantial evidence, in the area of peer tutoring for example, that these can be extremely effective. However the same issues of sex, personality and ability level still apply when deciding which children to group together.

Overall, we suggest some flexibility in group composition, since different tasks may demand different kinds of organisation. It seems important that the same groupings should be maintained at least over a series of sessions so that initial difficulties with cooperation can be overcome.

ACTIVITY 15

When you set up cooperative groupwork in the classroom, you will clearly have to make decisions about the make-up of groups. Making use of the information in this unit and your own experience, write notes on the kinds of attainment mix you would choose, the sex and personality mixes and the size of groups. Give reasons for your choices.

Unit 4

MANAGING GROUPS

PUPIL DEMANDS ON THE TEACHER'S TIME

Pupils make a great many demands on their teachers throughout the day. Consider this case-study of Matthew who is working by himself on a series of Maths tasks in a classroom where the majority of children seem interested in their work, are concerned with 'getting on' as fast as they can and are well acquainted with the classroom routines and the teacher's expectations. Although there are occasional arguments, particularly over necessary materials such as rubbers, the children are supportive and friendly towards the members of their group, helping when asked, voluntarily offering assistance, and organising each other.

However Matthew, an able seven year old, makes persistent demands on his teacher. (The following description is not a summary of all Matthew's activities, but shows the times of demands on the teacher in one lesson, as well as some explanation for them). Remember, too, that Matthew is just one from a class of thirty.

9.37 Matthew starts work on the first problem immediately, then stops to chat and look around the room. When the teacher approaches, he asks: 'Mrs Stevenson. Do you write the question?' The teacher replies: 'Yes if it's the sort where you write the question. Do you think you write the question?'

9.45 He then goes to the teacher to ask about the layout of the third question and is told to 'just do them underneath, like that'. He returns to his place, rapidly completes the multiplication tables and within two minutes has returned to the teacher, again asking about the layout. His work is marked and he goes back to his seat . . .

9.48 However, as soon as he has read the next question on his card, he gets up again, goes to the teacher . . .

9.57 He goes to ask the teacher where the weights are and is told: 'Oh, Miss Bradley's got them. Go and say, please Miss Bradley can we have our grams back . . .?' (he does so).

10.06 Matthew goes up to the teacher's desk and waits for a few minutes. He says, 'Mrs Stevenson, I've done the next column' and she asks him a series of questions about the work he has just completed . . .

10.21 He goes to the teacher's table.
Teacher: 'What does it say? . . .
(he has written the wrong answer)
Well, why have you put 1/2 to 3?
This writing's very poor. Come on.
Tell me what it says.'
He reads out the correct answer and is told to go and make his work a bit neater.

10.23 He rubs out some work and writes it neatly. Matthew goes back to the teacher.

ACTIVITY 16

Discuss the following:

1 What problems can you see in this extract in terms of classroom management? Remember that Matthew is one from a class of thirty others.
2 To what extent are Matthew's demands on the teacher necessary to his progress?
3 Do you experience similar problems with demands from pupils in your class?
4 In what ways might this pattern of demand be altered to allow the teacher more time for improved monitoring/unhurried explanation/ careful diagnosis of problems, and so on?

Using an observation schedule to monitor pupil demands

The teachers with whom we have been working have monitored the number and nature of demands on their time over several lessons by use of an observation schedule that they helped to develop. This is reproduced overleaf; each of the observation categories has an explanation and an illustration at the bottom of the sheet.

ACTIVITY 17

1 Using the observation schedule provided, familiarise yourself with the categories.
2 Fill in the demands on your time over a half hour period in the classroom during any lesson. The appropriate box should be ticked on each occasion that a child asks for your attention. The separation into five minute sections will serve as a rough guideline to time. An example of a completed schedule is shown below. (If these categories seem inappropriate, feel free to adapt or change them).
The teacher who completed this schedule describes how much of her time was taken up at the beginning of the lesson by children who had just started their Maths and came to her individually because they were unsure of how to organise their task. At the end of the period, these same children returned in order to have their work checked. Other demands were made on her by children working on a whole range of different writing activities.
3 Consider the nature and type of demands made on *you*, and the extent to which it was necessary for you to respond to them.

Pupil Demand Classification		TASK: Integrated Day (27 Demands) 0	5	10	15	20	PRE-GROUPING 25 – 30	TOTAL
1.	Instruction	✓✓		✓				3
2.	Presentation							
3.	Management i) Procedure			✓✓		✓✓	✓✓	6
4.	ii) Behaviour		✓	✓				2
5.	Evaluation i) interim	✓	✓✓✓✓✓ (MATHS)	✓	✓	✓		9
6.	ii) final				✓		✓✓✓ (END OF MATHS)	4
7.	Transitions				✓		✓	2
8.	Spellings	✓						1
9.	Materials							
10.	Routine							

Pupil Demand Classification		TASK:					PRE-GROUPING
		0	5	10	15	20	25 30
1.	Instruction						
2.	Presentation						
3.	i) Procedure Management						
4.	ii) Behaviour						
5.	i) interim Evaluation						
6.	ii) final						
7.	Transitions						
8.	Spellings						
9.	Materials						
10.	Routine						

1. Instruction – Relating to lack of, or misunderstanding of specific content or concept.
2. Presentation – Queries relating to what has to be done in content terms, i.e. to task instructions.
3. Management (i) Procedure – Relating to the manner of completion of work: 'Do I need a margin?'; 'Should I draw a graph or a table?'
4. Management (ii) Behaviour – 'Please Miss, John's kicking me'; 'The group is being silly'.
5. Evaluation (i) Interim – Requests for in-flight check. 'Am I doing it right?'
6. Evaluation (ii) final – End of task
7. Transitions – 'What should I do now?'
8. Spellings
9. Materials – 'Can I use the glue?'; 'Can I borrow a rubber?'
10. Routine – 'Can I go to the toilet?'

CREATING TIME – CHANGING PUPIL DEMANDS

The source of authority in the classroom is usually the teacher. It is hoped that in cooperative work, *the group* will become the initial source of reference for children, that they will turn first to their group, rather than the teacher, for their requests.

The teachers with whom we have worked have demonstrated that they can make time for themselves without allowing children to feel neglected, simply by being clearer to pupils about what demands they are willing to accept. If children are told explicitly, for example, that they must ask for help from their group before coming to the teacher, they seem prepared to accept this (though habit may need to be acquired through practice). The types of help needed will, of course, vary enormously but even young children can monitor the correctness or quality of each other's work, make decisions about materials, layout, sequence of work, and so on. The kind of task given to children is also likely to have an impact on the types of demand on the teacher.

One teacher describes how demand patterns can be almost instantly changed by asking children to refer to their group rather than to her. When she monitored two sessions she found that:

'. . . a total of 27 demands were made upon me during the space of 30 minutes during an integrated day. Of these 27 demands almost half, 13, in fact, were demands for me to evaluate partly completed or completed tasks. All demands were made by individual children needing help or reassurance about their own work.

During the second demand session there were far fewer demands made upon my time. During a half hour period there were only five requests made for interim evaluation, i.e. "Is this alright?"'

These children were aged seven to eight and were able to adjust their behaviour immediately when requested to do so. Of particular importance is

Freedom to teach a larger group, while the rest of the class work at cooperative tasks.

their teacher's claim that the quality of work was exceptionally good during this lesson, with the suggestion that most of the previous demands really had been unnecessary.

In a series of four lessons, another teacher of six to eight year olds found that demands dropped significantly, and, as illustrated below, many of the demands that were made *did* require her presence.

'Although the children had "spelling partners" and experienced encouragement to cooperate before the project began, there were twelve demands on my time in the first session.

In the second session there were three pupil demands, one came from Phillip, the youngest member of the highlighted group. His paper had fallen on the floor, and he came to tell me he had no paper.

One group leader was unsure of the task procedure, and one other child asked for the curtains to be drawn, because the sun was in her eyes.

In the third session one child had a nosebleed, and there were no other demands on my time.

In the fourth session, I walked around the classroom monitoring the groups, and, near the end of the lesson went to a group where one child was upset.

During the project the number of pupil demands fell away to almost zero. The children were clearly able to work well at their tasks without constant recourse to me and they showed clear benefits from the attitudes and skills they had acquired.'

These are not isolated cases of change in pupil behaviour, but serve as illustration of a general trend across all the classrooms in which we observed.

Clearly, after a while, teachers should find that they have considerable periods of time on their hands; they may at times become superfluous to the needs of the groups and will therefore be able to use their time for other activities, amongst which will need to be monitoring and assessment.

Despite teachers feeling guilty that they were not fulfilling their proper role (as we mentioned in the introduction to Unit 1) when they had time on their hands, they soon adjusted to using this time in different, and more useful, ways.

IMPROVING GROUPWORK THROUGH TRAINING

There seems to be an assumption among teachers that children do not need training in groupwork skills. Yet research, particularly in the United States, has shown that when such skills are practised the quality and effectiveness of groupwork improves, and many of the associated problems can be overcome by making children aware of the types of behaviour needed to operate successfully in groups. Training in the skills of groupwork might entail knowledge of how to listen, to question or to challenge within a group discussion; younger children can be encouraged to take a positive interest in the progress of their groups, to help each other, to ask clear questions, if necessary to persist in asking; all children can practise giving explanations of 'how' or 'why' rather than merely providing answers to be copied. Since we suggest that a major benefit of groupwork lies within the area of giving and receiving help, with the helpers clarifying their own understanding and the receiver hopefully benefitting from them, it is clearly important that pupils realise that the teacher values this behaviour. Too often we find that teachers who hold a strong *implicit* belief in cooperation fail to translate it into *explicit* expectations, or alternatively, fail to reward it appropriately.

As one teacher explains:

'Groupwork in itself is not an end to management problems, but will open up new ones, such as the ability to control the group's progress through a task, knowing when to intervene in matters of conflict or when the children cannot solve their differences, and in giving them support to complete tasks. To gain the best from groupwork I feel the teacher must train children to work in groups, to listen to each other, share ideas, work out problems together and maximise their learning.'

One teacher describes how she 'set out the ground rules' as follows:

'I felt that it was important to let the children know the aims of the task, and that discussion is an important skill. I told the children that I wanted to see if they could solve a problem by talking together, and to see if they could help each other work.

There were clear groupwork rules:

i) everyone must join in
ii) they must help each other
iii) they must not come to me unless there was a problem the group could not solve.

I used role play to emphasise help (rather than refusing), explaining (rather than giving a simple answer), being polite about asking for help and when receiving help, making eye contact, taking turns and listening to each other.

We discussed the benefits of helpful attitudes and skills such as sitting in a friendly formation, being supportive and the many benefits of working this way which the children and I perceived.

In future I would make it a much more positive policy to encourage and value helping and explaining skills, attitudes and values in my classroom. I would also aim to provide the children with feedback about those gains, so that they perceived the values and benefits of talking and cooperative skills.

When I asked the children why they worked in groups, they said:

- to practise getting on with one another
- to learn things other people know
- to get help with spellings
- to co-operate and help
- to listen to one another
- to think
- to solve problems
- to sort out what you will do.

Moving towards cooperation – training and practice

Cooperation does not always occur readily and groups do not always work easily together. Yet in our work with teachers we have seen that even over a short period of time during which cooperative effort is emphasised and valued, children will become more sensitive to the needs of the situation as we show below.

One headteacher rehearsed cooperative ways of working with a small group over a couple of weeks and then compared this group with others in his class.

Below is a short extract of talk from three children who had rehearsed cooperative ways of working.

Mark: I know. Cut some card off the corners.
Dawn: Yes.
Mark: So then we've got sort of shapes around the corner.
Dawn: Yeah, like round.
Mark: Yeah, or you could do it straight . . . Hey presto! Do it with a ruler . . . (watching Dawn using ruler) . . . In a bit, in a bit.
Patrick: That's not 13 (cms) yet, not quite.
Mark: That'll do . . . Yep, dead on.

This can be compared with talk from a group who are doing the same group task but who were not used to cooperating.

Paula: Anybody got 6 times 7?
Simon: Pardon?
Paula: Have you got 6 times 6?
Victoria: Paul, shall I do all of them yellow?
Paul: If you want.
Simon: What's eight 3's?
Paul: Simon, work it out for yourself.

ACTIVITY 18

Compare the two extracts of talk above by discussing the following questions:

1 What are the differences between them?
2 What kind of skills appropriate to cooperative groupwork do you think are evident in the first extract?
3 Do you agree with their teacher's comment that: 'Although one cannot claim that two such short extracts are wholly representative of the types of talk engaged in, I do feel that they provide indications as to the essential differences between the two groups.'?

Another teacher describes how eight to nine year olds in the group she is monitoring changed with respect to their behaviour, their language and their regard for each other over a period of several weeks during which they were asked to work together on different occasions.

'Since the aim was for the children to work cooperatively, the situation was created so that the emphasis was on cooperation between group members and not necessarily on finished product. Initially, children displayed a defensive attitude towards one another, ie. who was going to be dominant, who knew the answers, who was going to do the writing, who was going to let others do the finding out, etc.

This led to talk such as: 'No! I'm using them right now . . . look aren't I?'
'Well, nobody's going to use these ones because these are my personal property!. . .'

After a short time, observations made by the field worker and myself led us to believe that the children, on the whole, set aside preconceived ideas about who they thought should occupy certain status positions within the group.
In subsequent sessions children were much more relaxed. In time, they adopted different attitudes, shared their thoughts and began to recognise qualities in others.
'By the way you've got to make sure you cut it straight, exactly on the line.'
'Yes I will.'
'I don't know if mine's correct until I cut it out.'
'Kim, you've done that wrong, I'll give you a hand.'

A relationship built up over the weeks and in the last taped session some interesting language developed in terms of cooperation and positive regard for one another, including the use of "we" rather than "I".

Rebecca: Can I have the triangle please? Right . . . I've got some sellotape and I'm going to give her a hand.
Jordan: Thanks . . . just need to cut along this line.
Marie: I'll hold that for you while you draw around it. Remember what to do next? . . . Turn it over and let's see if we've got enough room here on the back . . . Now this time you'd better do the side first, make sure you've got enough room for the other sides . . . yeah you've got enough room.
Sam: Oh I know . . . oh yes. I see what to do . . . yeah thanks.
It wasn't quite straight . . . now it is.
(a minute later)
Marie: Done it Sam? That's right.'

Throughout this period, the teacher had continually emphasised appropriate behaviour and ways of working and the children responded readily to her demands.

ACTIVITY 19

Teachers will obviously need to consider ways of developing the helping behaviour that are so critical to effective groupwork. American researchers have developed strategies to help increase participation in groups. These are strategies that all teachers can use, as they feel appropriate. For example, the teacher says to her class:

A 'As I've been watching you work together, one thing I have noticed that people haven't been doing is (responding to requests for help, giving accurate explanations, encouraging other children etc). I want you to get better at this. Let's see if we can work out what you need to do.'

B 'I'd like each group to tell me how successful you have been at working together – and then we'll see if we can learn anything from each other.'

1. Do you think that these are useful ways of approaching the training of children in groupwork?
2. What alternatives can you think of that might improve on or extend the above examples?
3. Try out these, or similar, strategies with your own children as a starting point for evaluation.

ASSESSING GROUPWORK

MONITORING

The SEAC *Source Book of Teacher Assessment* (1990) makes specific reference to groupwork under the heading to Unit Four 'Monitoring performance'. They state that 'Groupwork requires the teacher to decide how best to manage and observe what is taking place' (4.1).

Observation is clearly central to the process of monitoring and SEAC suggest that teachers already often make use of observation. It may be part of everyday activity for many teachers who observe children constantly for evidence of, for example, progress, misunderstanding or developing relationships. However, if observation is to play a role in assessment of attainment, SEAC states:

Observation of process has to be planned for. Such observation for assessment should be analytical, moving beyond a general impression, into seeing what the child is actually doing. By being systematic in approach, familiarity with Statements of Attainment will increase.

Despite their often repeated pleas for a 'systematic approach', this is precisely what the SEAC document seems to lack in terms of groupwork, though much of what is stated is clearly important. Below, we reproduce a large part of the section on Groupwork, Assessing groupwork and Observation of interaction (4.12) so that you can consider these statements in the context of the knowledge you have gained by working through this booklet.

Groupwork
Effective groupwork is helped if:
- tasks lead to different kinds of output; for instance, tape recordings, models, a single report (spoken, written or otherwise) from the group, rather than relying on individual written records;
- tasks take place in different contexts (see Effect context on performance, 4.8);
- a realistic time scale is allowed for the group to perform;
- the teacher recognises there are some variables which cannot be controlled, such as weather, or a child having an 'off day';
- consideration has been given as to whether, to be effective, the task requires a mixed attainment group or a group of generally similar levels of attainment.

Assessing groupwork
To help assess the work of a group, a teacher needs to consider:
- how children share the tasks within the group;
- the level of involvement of individuals in the task;
- what kind of participation results in the task being taken forward;
- the kind of dialogue taking place: is talk centred on the task?
- how much time is spent off the task;
- how the teacher will approach observation (see Assessment techniques, 4.2).

Observation of interaction
Sharing and cooperation develop first in play situations. If an older child in primary school does not appear to be able to participate as intended, it may be a temporary effect due to the particular task, or one child may not relate well to another member of the group. Repeated observation will help a teacher to focus on causes, and indicate how help may be offered.

Current training activities in many schools and local education authorities are focusing on the observation of interaction.

It is recognised how difficult it may be to identify exactly how the interaction brings about learning. It may take time, as well as training and advice, for a teacher to develop full confidence in the observation of interaction.

Difficulty in assessing groupwork – a case study

Plan and participate in a presentation, e.g. of the outcome of a group activity, a poem, story, dramatic scene or play.

In order to assess this SoA, six children, who had been on a visit to the airport as part of a project on 'Flight', were asked to present an oral report to the class. As the group planned and carried out the presentation, the teacher observed them and recorded her observations on a check-list which included the features which had previously been identified as indicating attainment.

From the teacher's observations, it became clear that one member of the group dominated both the planning and presenting, whilst another remained passive, contributing little to the group discussion during planning and being content to participate as directed by the others.

The teacher expressed concern about her observations for these two individual children, because in designing the checklist such issues had not been taken into account. Furthermore the teacher was unclear as to how to relate performance of these children to the interpretation of the SoA. Both pupils had been involved in planning and participating but their degree of involvement was suspect and open to question in terms of interpersonal skills and group interaction. On the other hand, they had 'planned and participated in a presentation' and so, if the SoA was interpreted in a narrow sense, then they had satisfied the criteria for attainment.

This example demonstrates the need for a clear focus on the task, its demands and its relation to the criteria for assessment. Whilst assessment tasks should be clearly planned and structured it is necessary that teachers are adaptable in order to respond to pupil performance and behaviour which are not anticipated. (See Task setting, 4.7, and Group composition, 4.12).

ACTIVITY 20

1 Which of these SEAC statements do you find most useful in terms of enabling you to assess cooperative groupwork effectively? Why are they useful to you?
2 Taken together, do these statements prepare you adequately for assessment of groupwork?

You may have judged, as we have, that the SEAC statements are useful reminders of the many facets of groupwork, but do not make a significant contribution to assessment because they assume that, once prompted, the teacher is equipped to proceed.

Although teachers with whom we have worked have not yet observed specifically to ascertain whether children are able to achieve the required performance to pass an attainment target, it is clear that they do observe regularly and carefully.

One of these teachers suggests that it is possible to observe a group of children and assess:

'a) their ability to co-operate.
b) their understanding of the task and of how to implement its completion.
c) the suitability of the task in meeting their needs.
d) how the working group gels and how best its composition may be altered when necessary.
e) who is helping whom in each group and if the help is aiding the understanding of the task.
f) how suitable the resources available to learners are and how effectively the resources are used.'

However, the complexity of classroom situations, as this teacher admits, makes it difficult always to draw hard and fast conclusions about, for example, group relationships or learning.

Another teacher describes specific difficulties within groups that were picked up through observation:

'Sometimes a pupil may decide they cannot be bothered to work through things with a group. One of our pupils this year frequently showed that she wanted to get on with things in her own way. She made no fuss and did all the work necessary, sometimes doing everyone else's as well so that it could be done her way. As she was quietly industrious and as the other members in the group were happy to let her do it, this was not obvious unless we carefully watched the groups, as they worked . . .

Another boy opted out of his group accusing the others of not listening to him. I discussed both of these problems with the whole class to try to make the children realise that each of them had something to offer, that they should value each other and be able to feel a valued member of a group themselves.'

It would seem, from American evidence at least, that situations such as these are not unusual. Three kinds of pupil behaviour have been identified: 'free riders', 'suckers' and 'gangers'.

The 'free rider' effect

In certain types of task, especially when performance is dependent on high attaining children (for example, providing ideas for a joint essay), the less able may 'opt out' and simply go through the motions of groupwork without in fact making any real input. In other tasks, where a low attaining child is likely to hold back the whole group (for example, when cooperative group reading is slowed down by the poorest reader), it is the high attainers who are most likely to lose motivation, exert little effort and display the 'free rider' effect. Larger groups allow 'free riding' more easily than smaller ones.

The 'sucker' effect

Hard-working and motivated group members sometimes come to be less involved if they feel that others are taking advantage of them; that is, they avoid the 'sucker effect'. Thus, a child who is enthusiastic and full of ideas may gradually feel that her efforts are no longer worthwhile if others are not also willing to contribute effectively. Ineffective contributions may be judged in terms both of poor performance due to poor ability, or poor performance due to lack of effort.

Ganging up on the task

Children may also find ways round doing the task especially when they see it as pointless or simply do not like the work: 'my partner and I hate writing and we found ways to pretend that we are busy thinking about the essay'. This may also mean that part of the group do all the work on the assumption that: after all, if someone wants to do this task, they are welcome to do so, and if they need more help, then they have to negotiate.

Other effects

If children's attempted contributions are constantly rejected by the group, then they are unlikely to continue their efforts; alternatively, division of labour may emerge so that children do only what they are best at or most like.

In Britain, research on secondary children suggests possible problems with features such as those highlighted above. Other features to watch for are dominant pupils or those who fail to contribute over a long period of time; conflict in argument which becomes a slanging-match rather than a reflective activity; too much agreement without examining assumptions; problems associated with breaking away from 'habitual roles', for example, children failing to recognise that a 'class joker' may have a serious contribution, or that a poor reader may be an able problem solver.

It seems likely that any of these problems will emerge from time to time. If teachers are observant and notice the difficulties, it also seems likely that by making sure that children are aware of and understand the situation and by talking through the problem with the groups, the majority of issues can be resolved.

The links with 'training' children to work together can again be seen here, and it is clearly the teacher's observation of problems that will inform the kinds of training given in order, hopefully, to overcome them in the future.

Audio recordings

Teachers themselves suggest that their observations are not always adequate and that audio taped talk allows for different judgements:

'It is not always possible to observe a group closely, and I would have judged far more of the talk to be off-task than actually was.'

The best way of knowing how your pupils are participating and progressing is undoubtedly by listening to audio recordings of their talk, or perhaps video recording on occasion (though the soundtrack tends to be less good than that of audio recording which allows for better positioning of a microphone). We realise there can be difficulties associated with recording talk, especially when both pupils and teacher are unused to it, but children soon become used to the presence of a tape recorder and are quite able to use it appropriately.

Listening to a tape can provide many surprises for the teacher as well as being useful for the children themselves; children seem interested in and even prepared to discuss their own contributions, which may be important in the context of training for the teacher. Listening, obviously, takes time (though even a short drive home could be appropriate for this) but does not need to be done often in order to be of positive value.

Audio recording will also become an essential part of the 'evidence' needed to satisfy the demands of the National Curriculum for Speaking and Listening, along with short transcripts of talk which allow a deeper analysis. It may also provide data on 'particular words or moments which were revealing' (suggested by the Non-Statutory Guidance for Key Stage 1) over a range of activities.

Additionally, listening to talk can be a really pleasurable and even exciting activity for teachers who want to learn more about the children in their class, both in terms of the individual themselves and the ways in which groups can function. One teacher suggests:

'I have become aware that in examining the talk I have become more sensitive than formerly to the process by which children construct their meanings.'

Another teacher describes the detail which is available from listening to and transcribing talk:

'Transcripts showed the children to be patient, tolerant, honest, helpful, sometimes exasperated and relaxed. They were free to ask questions in a more informal atmosphere without embarrassment.

The children were able to co-operate with each other and allowed every group member to participate. I was especially pleased to find that the youngest child in my highlighted group was able to work so well in the group, and that the others were tolerant enough to modify their behaviour to take account of his relative immaturity. He was also able to talk without any embarrassment and showed no signs of talking in a muddled or stilted way.

I was surprised to find the extent to which the children gained skills in group management.

Some children adapted to working in groups more naturally than others. They had an instinctive awareness that they should sit in a friendly formation. They were able to listen to each other and take turns.'

A teacher of seven and eight year olds summarises:

'By reading the transcripts and listening to the tapes I realised how much young children can do by themselves. Whilst observing, I was occasionally tempted to intervene – had I done so I would have undoubtedly changed their course. In fact, they completed the task in the way they saw fit. It is likely that they gained more from following their own course than from taking the lead from me. I hope I will be less ready to criticise what I see as irrelevant contributions or material in the future, and so give more opportunities for this kind of undirected work.

By maintaining a low profile I was hopefully encouraging the children to become self-reliant rather than teacher-dependent. The children were extremely capable and mostly willing to help each other and were actively promoting each other's learning. They certainly didn't need me to answer low-level requests. The responsibility for success relied on the children participating together. With this came the realisation that my presence was not necessarily required for learning to take place.'

Listening to tapes also allows teachers to know whether the concern outlined below is, indeed, a rightful concern, or simply a theoretical possibility:

'There is perhaps a danger that the less able children are not doing very much and are being overlooked by the teacher because they are not demanding much attention either. It seems evident that just because a group produces a successful end product does not mean all have participated fully, and that there is a need for careful monitoring of the work of each individual.'

ACTIVITY 21

When you have set up cooperative groups (as we hope you will do when you have completed this workbook), audio-tape a group of your choice during a lesson and listen to the recording. Are you surprised by the ways in which children work together, or fail to cooperate? Do any of the pupils perform in ways you did not anticipate?

If your children do not yet work cooperatively but you are interested in children's talk, record a lesson now, or at any time, and compare talk from a lesson where cooperation is not emphasised, either by the task or by the teacher, with one when it is.

MODES OF ASSESSMENT

Much of what is important in cooperative groupwork can only be assessed during the process. Audio tapes are particularly useful since they allow for a clear insight into this process, and for this reason discussion of them is included under 'monitoring'. They do, however, also allow for assessment of that process after the event. Yet often, a teacher will need to assess groupwork after a task has been completed and will have no record of the process, either from an audio-tape or from close observation. We now discuss ways in which this can be done.

1 For tasks with an end product

Tasks of this nature might be: making an artefact such as a model, a piece of writing or a drawing.

When *individual end products* are demanded by the task, even though the children are working as a group, it is clear that each child's work can be assessed individually. The only problems with the assessment of this individual work are that some pupils may copy others, or lean heavily on others' ideas without producing their own.

When *joint end products* are demanded by the task, individual assessment is more difficult.

The proof of the pudding . . . . . .!

Individual accountability is low and it is difficult for the teacher to know what each child has contributed.

There are several methods by which teachers can gain more information about the ways in which children worked at the task which will in turn inform their assessment of the end product.

i) *Post task interviews* with individuals or groups will enable teachers to ascertain the degree of participation and understanding of each child, the nature of support to, or from, others, etc.
ii) *Whole class discussion* allows teachers to review a task as children report back on their activities and reflect on their work; end products can be compared or analysed critically and pupils' responses will indicate their degree of involvement in, and understanding of, the task.
iii) Post task written tests (or drawings) demonstrate the extent to which individual children have learned or understood specific features relating to the task they have just completed. The written product is easily assessed.

2 For tasks without an end product

(that is, discussion tasks)

Tasks without an end product, that is, discussion tasks are always dependent on *joint participation* in the development of ideas, the airing of opinions, the raising of arguments, and so on. Although monitoring of the process itself will always give the most information, the same methods as those given above will be appropriate for gathering feedback from the pupils as to how they tackled the task.

i) *Post task interviews* with individuals, groups or the whole class,
ii) *Whole class discussion* in which teachers can review arguments, investigate hypotheses, consider ideas and understand how conclusions were reached. In short, the children enable the teacher to take part in the process of their discussions, but retrospectively.
iii) *Post-task writing (or drawing)*: The discussion task may be followed up by a piece of writing or a drawing: an end product produced either individually or jointly. Often this is integral to the task and assessed in its own right.

Below are presented some teachers' accounts to illustrate i) to iii) above.

i) Post task interviews

Interviews with children after completing their tasks can take different forms and are used for different purposes. This is shown below by the ways in which two different teachers talk to their children.

A teacher who asked groups of six and seven year olds to build a shelter out of Quadro deliberately did not involve herself with the children during the task. Her interviews, however, demonstrate to them that she is interested in both their groups and what they have done, as well as telling her about the level of participation of each child and whether they were satisfied with the group's end product.

These were actually individual interviews, but similar questions would be appropriate for groups or even a class.

Teacher: You all made a lovely house today. Which parts of it did you build?

Sarah: Well I decided to build in the ladder and two windows. I helped Leanne to build the windows, and I helped the little square that we did first.

Gemma: I did a couple of the top bits. I did some of the starting bits where you make it up and the bottom bit some of the side bit.

Teacher: If you could go and spend longer on it would you make any changes to it?

Anthony: Yes. Well that straight bit, you know when Benjamin had that long bit where two bits went in, and I said 'Ben I don't think that will work', because there wasn't a bit like it on the other side, well I would change that bit.

Benjamin: Well, I'd just make it look a bit, a lot better.

Teacher: How would you do that?

Benjamin: Well, so, just. Just imagine that Robinson Crusoe had to stay in it for a night, right, well I'd make it longer. I'd make the sides longer and I'd make it a bit taller.

In post task interviews it is also possible to assess progress and learning. With older children (ten year olds), a teacher interviews a group about a poem they have been reading and illustrating by themselves, so that he can check for their attempts at meaning-making and understanding. The task had been set as a cooperative problem-solving activity and this interview demonstrates the continuation of a sharing process with the pupils themselves taking on a questioning role and the teacher's presence barely necessary, except to confirm his interest in the children. He is thus able to concentrate fully on the talk, their reaching for meaning and the understanding which they relate to their own personal experiences. Part of the interview is given below:

Discussion of 'The Forest of Tangle'

Teacher: Did you enjoy the poem?
(Pause)
Samantha: I like it, he sounds like a nice man.
Mary-Anne: So do I, he likes animals and he lives with them so that he can make them better.
Matthew: He's on his own, he's lonely.
Mary-Anne: He's got the animals but he cried – he was crying because he was on his own.
Neil: He's the King . . . (Pause) Kings are lonely.
Teacher: What do you think he was doing?
Matthew: Crying – he was crying.
(Indistinct, several voices)
Mary-Anne: He was alone and he helped the animals in the forest, he had lots of things for them, to help them.
Samantha: He didn't sell them because no one came, he was like a . . . maker who can't sell what he makes.
Mary-Anne: He made things for people but they didn't come, he made all sorts of things.
Matthew: He made animals with the bits, he was making animals from all the different parts.
Neil: Is he a god? Is the King of the makers a god?
Mary-Anne: He is sort of . . . like that because he made lots of things.
Samantha: If he is a god why does he cry, why is he crying?
Matthew: Because
Neil: I know
Matthew: Because he's making (Indistinct, several voices)
(Pause)
Mary-Anne: He's making the world and he doesn't know why.

ii) Whole class discussion

A teacher explains how she brought the class together at the end of each cooperative groupwork class. Her pupils were aged between six and eight, but this form of organisation lends itself to children of any age.

'I deliberately designed the tasks so that there was no obvious solution for each problem. There was never an occasion when each group came to the same decision. This, I believe, shows that the problems were open- ended. It also meant that the class discussion after each session was broad and lively.

After each groupwork task, the whole class came together to talk about their solutions to the problems. On each occasion I asked a quiet or low ability child from each group to explain their group decision. They were always able to do so. This showed that in each group the children were able to explain the decision the group had come to, they were therefore all involved in the learning in each task.'

It is interesting that in both post task interviews and class follow-up periods there is some evidence of teachers promoting talk particularly in terms of abstract ideas, taking up decisions made by children and questioning and challenging. For example, those children who had been making carts with wheels and bodies of different shapes and sizes were fully aware of the proportions of their own group's product. The teacher-led discussion as to why some carts rolled further or faster than others now became meaningful to every child as they realised exactly how their own group's cart was different from another's; pupils were prepared to argue the strengths and weaknesses of their own cart.

The prospect of achieving greater understanding in children through assessment procedures is an interesting and, potentially, very fruitful one.

iii) Post task written tasks (or drawings)

Several teachers gave their groups both pre task and post task written tests. An example is given below. The task which had been set for the groups was purely practical in that it demanded making cubes, but their teachers wanted to know about the knowledge of cubes these children possessed before the task and the extent to which a practical activity might extend this knowledge. One teacher reports:

'The group seem to have had a fairly accurate idea of objects they thought were cubes before the task. All except one child thought the faces of a cube are the same in the pre-task test. She had changed this assumption by the post-task test and she too agreed that all the faces of a cube are the same. None attempted to draw a net before the task in the pre-task test, but all produced fairly accurate ideas on the net of a cube in the post-task test. These are the nets they produced.'

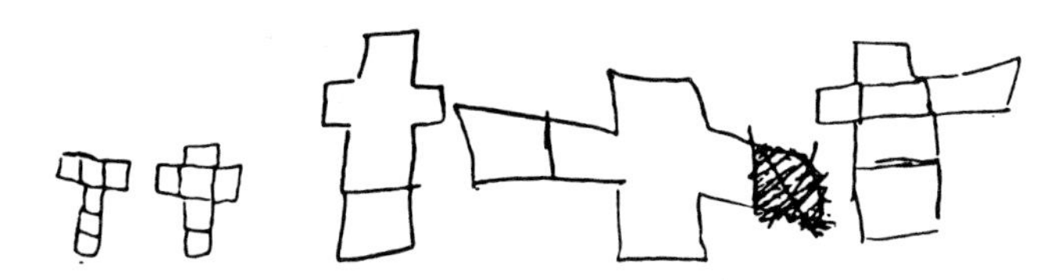

From these nets, the teacher is able to ascertain both the children's progress and understanding, and also that the task set achieved what she had intended, that is, that the children should be able to draw nets of cubes.

ACTIVITY 22

Discuss the following questions:

1 In what ways do you assess children at present?
2 Do you assess pupils in any of the ways suggested here, If yes, in what circumstances do you do so and why? If no, decide which method you find of most interest and plan how you could implement it with children.

We will ask you to consider assessment again at the end of the workbook and when you have set up cooperative groups in the classroom.

Unit 6

IMPLEMENTATION OF COOPERATIVE GROUPWORK IN THE CLASSROOM

The previous sections and activities will – we hope – have made you aware of the issues, practicalities and problems surrounding the implementation of cooperative groupwork. To summarise, you need to be clear about:

i) The groupwork task, in terms of cooperation and talk as well as the subject content.

ii) The ways in which you will ask the groups to behave and how you will encourage them to work and talk together.

iii) The extent to which you will hand over 'authority' to the group in order to create more time for yourself; and what you will do with this time.

Emergent writing: first year infants write notes as they listen to a tape of 'The Sea'. Ideas will be shared in a 'joint' discussion.

ACTIVITY 23

This activity is designed to help you set up groupwork in the classroom.

We provide you with a 'Planning Guide' below. Answering the questions will help you to focus on the aspects of your practice that will need attention in order to implement cooperative groupwork. The format allows you to plan for one lesson or session only, but can be photocopied for further tasks. It is also possible that the answers relating to questions 1-3 and 5-12 may remain constant for a period of time, whilst the specific content of the children's task (question 4) will change.

1 On which curriculum area are you going to concentrate?

2 With which attainment targets will you deal?

3 On which specific statement(s) of attainment will you concentrate?

4 What is the actual task you want the children to work at?

5 Which model of grouping are you going to adopt?

6 Does the task fit the group model? How does it do so? For example, is individual accountability built in if you are going to use the 'jigsaw' approach?

7 Are you going to ask the whole class to work in cooperative groups, or just part of the class?

8 How are you going to compose your groups? Why did you come to this decision?

9 What expectations do you have for group behaviour and cooperation? How will you inform the groups about this?

10 Will you ask the groups to take first responsibility for pupil requests?
How will you monitor whether this happens?

11 What use will you make of your time if you are free from constant demands, for example, observation of specific children or assessment of progress?

12 How will you record children's performances?

Right, you are now ready to implement cooperative grouping. Set a time and a date – and go for it!

ACTIVITY 24

As soon as you feel ready you will need to observe the frequency and type of pupil demands again to ascertain if, and how, these have changed. For this purpose we have reproduced another copy of the observation schedule overleaf.

Compare your two lessons in terms of their differing patterns. Are there significant differences in the quantity, or type of demand? What are they?

If you have a colleague who is carrying out the same exercise, compare your findings.

ACTIVITY 25

Finally, in Unit 5 we asked you to record the talk of one group. Do this as soon as you feel that the group is ready for it and don't worry if your first recording is not particularly successful; just try again!

Listen to the talk yourself. You may also find it appropriate to allow the children to listen to themselves. They are often as surprised as you at the ways in which they participate and may also learn from the experience.

Discussion with your colleagues about groupwork experiences (both successes and failures) will alert you to means for further progress and possibilities. We hope that you will continue to refine your practice as regards cooperative groupwork and that over a period of time, whole-school policies will serve to strengthen all initiatives in this area.

Pupil Demand Classification		TASK: 0–5	5–10	10–15	15–20	20–25	POST-GROUPING 25–30
1.	Instruction						
2.	Presentation						
3.	Management i) Procedure						
4.	Management ii) Behaviour						
5.	Evaluation i) interim						
6.	Evaluation ii) final						
7.	Transitions						
8.	Spellings						
9.	Materials						
10.	Routine						

1. Instruction – Relating to lack of, or misunderstanding of specific content or concept.
2. Presentation – Queries relating to what has to be done in content terms, i.e. to task instructions.
3. Management (i) Procedure – Relating to the manner of completion of work: 'Do I need a margin?'; 'Should I draw a graph or a table?'
4. Management (ii) Behaviour – 'Please Miss, John's kicking me'; 'The group is being silly'.
5. Evaluation (i) Interim – Requests for in-flight check. 'Am I doing it right?'
6. Evaluation (ii) final – End of task
7. Transitions – 'What should I do now?'
8. Spellings
9. Materials – 'Can I use the glue?'; 'Can I borrow a rubber?'
10. Routine – 'Can I go to the toilet?'

FURTHER READING AND REFERENCES

Further Reading

There is a wide-ranging and easily available literature on children's talk. A text which develops important ideas about the role of talk in learning from infancy to the end of primary education is *The Meaning Makers* by Gordon Wells (see *References* below). He particularly suggests ways in which adults, especially teachers, can foster knowledge and understanding in children, and his ideas about 'meaning-making' through talk are also central to our own arguments for learning in groups.

Practical texts on cooperative learning are harder to come by. There are two useful and easy to read texts which we recommend, despite the fact that the former discusses secondary age children and the latter is set in the American context. Both, however, are full of discussion, strategies for management, reviewing of problems and are firmly based in classrooms.

1 Cowie and Rudduck (see below)
2 Cohen, E G (1986) *Designing Groupwork – Strategies for the Heterogeneous Classroom* New York and London: Teachers College Press

References

Alexander, R (1984) *Primary Teaching* New York and London: Holt, Rinehart and Winston

Assessment of Performance Unit: Speaking and listening (1986) Assessment at Age 11.

Bennett, S N and Cass, A (1988) The Effects of Group Composition on Group Interactive Processes & Pupil Understanding *British Educational Research Journal*, 15, 19-32

Bennett, N; Desforges, C; Cockburn, A and Wilkinson, B (1984) *The Quality of Pupil Learning Experiences* London: Laurence Erlbaum Associates

Bennett, N and Dunne, E (1989) *'Implementing Cooperative Groupwork'*, paper presented at EARLI Conference, Madrid.

Bullock Report (1975) *A Language for Life* London: HMSO

Cockroft Report (1982) *Mathematics counts:* report of the Committee of Enquiry into Teaching of Mathematics in Schools London: HMSO

Cowie, H and Rudduck, J (1988) *Cooperative Groupwork – An Overview* B P Educational Service for Sheffield University

DES (1989) *Task Group on Assessment and Testing A Report*

DES (1989) *National Curriculum – English 5-11* London: HMSO

Dunne, R (in press) *Assessment for Learning* Macmillan Education

Galton, M; Simon, B and Croll, P (1980) *Inside the Primary Classroom* London: Routledge and Kegan Paul

HMI (1978) *Primary Education in England* London: HMSO

HMI (1983) 9-13 *Middle Schools: An Illustrative Survey* London: HMSO

HMI (1985) *Education 8-12 in Combined and Middle Schools* London: HMSO

HMI (1989a) *Aspects of Primary Education – Teaching and Learning of Maths* London: HMSO

HMI (1989b) *Aspects of Primary Education – Teaching and Learning of Science* London: HMSO

Johnson, D and Johnson, R (1975) *Learning Together and Alone* Englewood Cliffs: Prentice Hall

Kagan, S (1988) *Cooperative Learning: Resources for Teachers* University of California, Riverside

National Oracy Project (1989) *Talk: the Journal of the National Oracy Project* No 1 London: NCC

NCC (1989) English in the National Curriculum Key Stage 1. York: NCC.

Plowden Report (1967) *Children and their Primary Schools* London: HMSO

SEAC (1990) A Source Book of Teacher Assessment, Pack C from *A Guide to Teacher Assessment* Heinemann Education on behalf of SEAC London: Heinemann

Schmuck (1985) in Slavin, R E (ed) *Learning to cooperate, cooperating to learn* New York: Plenum

Slavin, R E (1983) *Cooperative Learning* New York: Longman

Vygotsky, L S (1962) *Thought and Language* Cambridge: M.I.T. Press

Webb, N (1982) *Peer Interaction and learning in Cooperative Groups* paper presented at AERA Conference, New York

Wells, G (1987) *The Meaning Makers: Children Learning Language and Using Language to Learn* London, Sydney, Auckland, Toronto: Hodder and Stoughton

Wragg, E C; Bennett, S N and Carré C G (1989) Primary teachers and the National Curriculum *Research Papers in Education*, 4, 3.